Study career perceptions Hospitality Industry

By,
Sharma, Manish Kumar

ACKNOWLEDGEMENT

At the outset, I would like to express my sincere gratitude to my Supervisor, Dr Ankur Kumar Agarwal for giving me the opportunity to work in this area. It would never be possible for me to take this Ph.D. thesis to this level without his continuous support, motivation, patience and technical advice. I would not have accomplished this task. Throughout my thesis-writing period, he provided encouragement, sound advice, good teaching, good company and lots of good ideas that I would have missed without him.

I would like to convey my sincere thanks to Prof. KVSM Krishna, Vice Chancellor, Prof. J.L Jain (Dean Faculty of Humanities) Prof. Rajeev Sharma, Prof. Anurag Shakya, Prof. Siddharth Jain and Prof. Saurabh Kumar for their continuous support, suggestions and encouragement for completing this thesis work.

A special to thanks my family, words cannot express how grateful I am to my mothers Smt. Bina Sharma and Smt. Chitralekha Kaushik. I would like to convey a special thanks to my wife Mrs. Shikha for her unstinted support and patience as also to my daughter Raisha Sharma and my son Achyut Sharma.

(Manish Kumar Sharma)
Enrolment No. 20181080

TABLE OF CONTENTS

Candidate's Declaration…………………………………………………… i
Certificate of the Guide………………………...…………………………… ii
Acknowledgement…………………………………………………………… iii
List of Publications………………………………………………………… iv
Abstract…………………………………………………………………… v
List of Table………………………………………………………………… vi
List of Figures……………………………………………………………… viii
List of Abbreviations……….…..…………………………………………… ix

CHAPTER – I 1
1 INTRODUCTION 1
   1.1   The Chapter's Introduction 1
   1.2   Background 1
      1.2.1   The Hotel Industry 1
      1.2.2   The Indian Hotel Industry 3
      1.2.3   Hospitality In the World 4
      1.2.4   Emergence of Hotel Services 5
      1.2.5   Hotel Services 7
      1.2.6   Employment Generation in India... 7
      1.2.7   Tourism and Hospitality Industry Growth and Development........ 8
      1.2.8   Role of Hotel Management Courses in Hospitality sector.......... 10
      1.2.9   Role of the Multinational Companies 11
   1.3   Introduction to Recruitment and Career Advancement: 11
      1.3.1   Concept of Recruitment: 13
      1.3.2   Concept of Career: 13
      1.3.3   Growth & Development of the Concept of Career: 14
      1.3.4   Career Path 16
      1.3.5   Progression In the Career... 17
      1.3.6   Obstacles To Career Progression 18
      1.3.7   Strategies For Advancing Your Career 19
      1.3.8   Career Advancement Theories 20

	1.3.9	Career Advancement:	24
	1.3.10	Career Advancement/Development Required:	25
1.4		Career Development Approaches	27
	1.4.1	Organizational Strategy	27
1.5		Self-Efficacy: An Overview:	30
	1.5.1	Occupational Attitudes:	31
	1.5.2	Awareness of Oneself:	31
1.6		The Hotel's Employees	32
	1.6.1	Performance of Employees	33
	1.6.2	Employee Perceptions of Their Work	33
1.7		Problem Statement for Research	33
1.8		The Study's Purpose	34
1.9		Research Questions	34
1.10		Significance Of the Study	35
1.11		Research Objectives	35
1.12		Limitation	36
1.13		Summary Of the Chapters	36
CHAPTER – II			**38**
2 LITERATURE REVIEW			38
2.1		Career Decision-Making: A Conceptual Framework	38
2.2		Career-Decision-Making Theoretical Approaches	39
	2.2.1	Career Decision-Making Psychological Approaches	40
	2.2.2	Research on Theories of Career Choice	42
	2.2.3	Perspectives of Employee	43
	2.2.4	Employee' Perspective on Job satisfaction and Career Progression	45
	2.2.5	Employee's Perspective on Employee's Benefits and Career Progression	48
	2.2.6	Employee's Perspective on Technological Advancement and Career Progression	50
	2.2.7	Concept of Employee Workload and Job Satisfaction	50
	2.2.8	Workload Perception and Employees' Areas of Specialisation	51
2.3		Women Employee' Perception for Career Progression	53
	2.3.1	Women Employee' Perception about Career in the Hotel Industry	53
2.4		Student Perspective	54
	2.4.1	Students' Internship Experiences and Impact on Career Decision Making	57

    2.4.2   Students' Perspective on Social Status and Their Impact on Career Decision Making 59
- 2.5 The Impact of Culture on Career Perceptions 60
- 2.6 The Impact of Job satisfaction on Career Perception....................................62
- 2.7 Employees of the Hotel Industry...65
  - 2.7.1 The Significance of Human Resource Management in Hotels..............65
  - 2.7.2 Improving Service Quality via Employee Management and Skill Development ....
  - 2.7.3 Employee Empowerment's Impact on the Hotel Industry 68
- 2.8 Employees Performance..68
  - 2.8.1 Employee performance effectiveness in terms of service quality 68
  - 2.8.2 Hospitality Management Employee Motivation and Performance........69
- 2.9 Conclusion...71

CHAPTER –III 73
3 RESEARCH METHODOLOGY 72
- 3.1 Introduction 72
- 3.2 Research Design 72
- 3.3 Data Collection Methods...73
  - 3.3.1 Primary Data 73
  - 3.3.2 Secondary Data 73
- 3.4 Sample Design...73
  - 3.4.1 Target Population...74
  - 3.4.2 Sampling Frame and Sampling Location...74
  - 3.4.3 Sampling Elements 75
  - 3.4.4 Sampling Techniques...75
  - 3.4.5 Sampling Size 75
- 3.5 Research Instrument..76
  - 3.5.1 Pilot Study..76
  - 3.5.2 Full Study...77
- 3.6 Constructs Measurement (Scale and Operational Definitions).....................78
- 3.7 Data Processing 86
- 3.8 Data Analysis 87
  - 3.8.1 Descriptive analysis 87
  - 3.8.2 Scale Measurement – Reliability Test 88
  - 3.8.3 Inferential Analysis..89

3.9 Conclusion 91
CHAPTER – IV 93
4 DATA ANALYSIS 92
    4.1 Introduction 92
    4.2 Descriptive Analysis 92
        4.2.1 Demographic Profile of Respondents 92
    4.3 Descriptive Analysis (Interns-Students) 101
        4.3.1 Gender 101
        4.3.2 Work Experience 102
        4.3.3 Year of Study 103
        4.3.4 Willingness To Work in Industry 104
    4.4 Central Tendencies Measurement of Constructs 104
    4.5 Scale Measurement 116
        4.5.1 Internal Reliability Test 116
        4.5.2 Test of Data Normality 117
    4.6 Factor Analysis 123
        4.6.1 KMO Test and Bartlett's Test of Sphericity to Check Adequacy Of Sample……………………………………………………..123
        4.6.2 Confirmatory Factor Analysis – Structural Equation Modelling 125
    4.7 Inferential Analyses 128
        4.7.1 Pearson Correlation Coefficient 128
        4.7.2 Multiple Regression Analyses 133
    4.8 Variables Affecting Employee' Perceptions Toward the Hospitality Industry as a Career Choice 134
    4.9 Conclusion 138
CHAPTER – V 140
5 SUMMARY OF RESULTS 139
    5.1 Introduction 139
    5.2 Summary of Statistical Analyses 139
        5.2.1 Summary of Descriptive Analyses 139
        5.2.2 Normality Test 141
        5.2.3 Factor Analysis 142
        5.2.4 KMO Test and Bartlett's Test of Sphericity to Check Adequacy Of Sample…. 142
        5.2.5 Reliability Test 143
        5.2.6 Confirmatory Factor Analysis – Structural Equation Modelling 143

- 5.3 Inferential Analyses 143
  - 5.3.1 Pearson Correlation Analyses 143
  - 5.3.2 Multiple Regression Analyses 146
- 5.4 Variables Affecting Employee' Perceptions Toward the Hospitality Industry as a Career Choice 146
- 5.5 Conclusion 148

CHAPTER – VI 150
- 6 DISCUSSION AND CONCLUSION 149
  - 6.1 Discussion And Conclusions 149
    - 6.1.1 Findings & Conclusions On The Basis Of Research Objective – 1: ... 149
    - 6.1.2 Findings & Conclusions On The Basis Of Research Objective- 2: 150
    - 6.1.3 Findings & Conclusions On The Basis Of Research Objective- 3 And 4 152
    - 6.1.4 Findings & Conclusions On The Basis Of Research Objective- 5: 153
  - 6.2 Limitation of the Study 156
  - 6.3 Recommendations for Future Research 156
  - 6.4 Conclusion 157
- 7 REFERENCES 159
- 8 APPENDICES 182
  - 8.1 Questionnaire For Employees 182
  - 8.2 Questionnaire For Students 185
  - 8.3 Research Papers 190

CHAPTER – I

1 INTRODUCTION

1.1 The Chapter's Introduction

Employees play a critical part in providing services to clients or travellers visiting hotels in any economy **(Chen, 2013)**. The introductory chapter provides a brief summary of the study topic as well as the reasoning for selecting it as a thesis topic. In this chapter, the hotel business and its characteristics are discussed, as well as the recruitment and career advancement of hotel's professionals for their career progression. The problem statement illustrates the major difficulties surrounding the research thesis subject. This chapter also discusses the research thesis's objectives and the importance of the thesis paper in understanding the relevance of employees' perceptions of career advancement and performance in enhancing the standard of service in the Indian hotel industry. As a result, the study aims to uncover characteristics that might inspire employees to improve their performance. The research hypothesis is framed around these study aims. This chapter presents the research questions that the researcher will answer throughout the writing of the thesis paper. The thesis' limits, as well as the paper's general framework or summary, are discussed in the last portion of this chapter.

1.2 Background

1.2.1 The Hotel Industry

A hotel is a professional facility or organisation that charges guests for the privilege of staying overnight. Tourist facilities and services can differ greatly from one hotel to the next, and hotel owners generally tailor their pricing and marketing strategies to appeal to a certain type of customer.

The hotel business is one of the most significant components of the broader service industry, providing to clients that need overnight lodging. It is closely connected with the travel and hospitality industries, however, there are significant distinctions in scope. Due to their nature, hotel services are inextricably linked to the travel and tourism industries. Most definitions of the hotel business include hostels, motels, inns, and guest homes in addition to hotels. On the other hand, long-term or permanent housing is frequently excluded.

Following that, you must reply to the inquiry, "What is the hotel industry?" You may be wondering. Simply put, the hotel sector is a branch of the service industry that deals with guest accommodations. By most definitions, the hotel sector includes not just hotels, but also hostels, motels, inns, and guest homes, as well as other forms of overnight lodging. It does not, however, generally comprise long-term or permanent accommodations.

Hotel services are intimately related to the travel and tourism sector due to their nature.

This hotel industry is an undivided part of the service industry. The researcher will provide an idea about the service industry in the latter part of the thesis but services have been interpreted as actions, performances, operations, or procedures by a number of academics. Services, according to **(Parasuraman, 1985)**, are invisible, perishable, inseparable, and heterogeneous behavioural entities. These characteristics mean that a company's services cannot be reliably calculated and sustained **(Harvey, 1998)**. The main issue here is that management must ensure that overall service efficiency maximises benefits while lowering costs.

Many individuals misunderstand the hotel and hospitality industries, assuming they are the same. While there is some overlap, the hospitality industry is far broader and includes a wide range of businesses. The hotel industry is solely dedicated to providing accommodation and other tourist-related services. In contrast, the hotel sector is largely focused with leisure in a broad sense. Hotels, restaurants, bars, cafés, nightlife, and a variety of travel and tourist services are all covered as a consequence.

The consistency of a service is determined not just by the performance, but also by the processes and techniques used to provide the service. This idea is supported by a large number of scholars **(Bolton and Drew, 1991); (Weng, 1994)**.

1.2.2 The Indian Hotel Industry

With guest homes in the Himalayas, royal hotels in Rajasthan, creative, specialised hotels in one of the megacities, beach resorts in Goa, and houseboats in Kerala, India has something for everyone, from backpackers to wellness tourists to business travellers. In recent years, both worldwide tourist arrivals and local tourism have risen. The latter, in particular, holds out hope for the hotel business in 2021, given the low number of international travellers predicted.

After The Beatles' trip to Rishikesh in 1968, which ushered in the first wave of international tourists to India, tourism and hospitality did not pick up until the early 1990s, after market liberalizations.

Since 2000, India's hotel business has developed significantly, owing to the country's attractiveness to travellers from all over the world. India receives around 2.1 per cent of all foreign tourism revenues and is the most popular tourist destination in the world, according to tourists (Tourism Alliance, 2014). India's tourism industry is one of the most important employers in the country, accounting for 7.6% of total employment. As a result, India's hospitality and tourist sector has had the fastest growth in terms of employment. In 2017, India's hotel sector was massive, with about 162.000 five-star hotels. This is an increase over the previous year's figure of 136.000 units. The statistics peaked at 162.000 Units in 2017 and peaked at 54.000 Units in 1998, respectively. In CEIC, data with a five-star rating is still active (Ministry of Tourism). However, in order to maintain the hotel industry's development, hoteliers must place a premium on the service quality and degree of customer satisfaction that guests experience throughout their stay.

The average daily rate (ADR) by room, revenue per available room (RevPAR), and occupancy rate are all important metrics in this market. The average room rate had been unstable even before the coronavirus (COVID-19) epidemic. Five-star hotels, for example, peaked in 2011 at 140 dollars per night, before falling to 93 dollars per night in 2019. In recent years, both the RevPAR rate and the occupancy rate have changed.

In India, the year 2020 began with favourable conditions for hotels. Due to the coronavirus (COVID-19) pandemic, the government instituted a lockdown and harsh travel restrictions in late March 2020. Despite the fact that the whole sector is still dealing with the ramifications, there were rays of hope: domestic demand boosted firms over the holiday season near the end of 2020, and brief staycations became a new fad for weary city inhabitants following the lockdown.

In 2019, India's government cut the goods and services tax (GST) on hotels in order to boost the country's competitiveness. During the pandemic, the government also created the "Dekho apna desh" webinar series, as well as the SAATHI assessment and awareness campaign, to boost domestic travel (System for Assessment, Awareness and Training for Hospitality Industry). Business travel was expected to take a back seat in the near future due to increased digitalization and most companies' expanded work-from-home policy, enabling leisure travellers to take their place.

1.2.3 Hospitality In the World

The hotel industry is predicted to increase at an annual pace of 8% to $5,891 billion by 2022. Future growth will be fueled by both economic progress and technical improvements in industrialised countries. Compass Group PLC, Marriott International, Starbucks Coffee, Sodexo, Aramark Corporation, McDonald's, Hilton Worldwide, Chick-fil-A, and Elior Group are among the market's top players. The company – career opportunities in the travel and hospitality industry are rapidly growing and putting in long hours **(Kusluvan and Kusluvan, 2000)**. Because of the service-oriented nature of the industry, some experts believe that trained, knowledgeable, passionate, and devoted employees are needed to ensure high service standards. However, the sector globally faces a qualified labour shortage, which may be addressed by examining education and training. It might be possible to draw assumptions on what needs to change to promote a transition in order to remedy the shortage of expertise by attempting to consider students' views of tourism and hospitality. A variety of negative characteristics draw graduates and/or a skilled workforce to the industry's challenges. According to **(Baum, 2006),** there is an unbroken loop in which persons that the company is involved in are not hired by the industry but are unfairly open to it. However, the image and the facts are not always the same. The concept of "extremely desirable, secure, career-based, clustered and/or part-time and shift-work jobs in the tourism and hospitality industry" **(Collier and Harraway, 2003)**.

Since several professions are considered glamorous and exhilarating, **(Baum, 2006)** points out that there is a conservative and glamorous attitude to the negative perception of the company. E.g. he employs aeroplane agents. Furthermore, when analysing these remarks, it is important to consider the data collection method, since it does not represent the entire industry. Only the worst bosses, for example, can be prosecuted. Although the industry is often described as requiring a low degree of expertise, there is evidence to the contrary. Because of the diversity of positions in the sector, it's challenging to describe low-skilled work because some of them need a high degree of experience, such as airline pilots and museum curators. Because of the wide range of careers available in the tourism and hospitality sectors, the sector needs a diverse set of skills and when this is mixed with low entrance barriers, career rivalry is fierce **(Szivas and Riley, 2002)**. Despite this proof, the industry still has a shortage of qualified labour and a negative picture of the work.

1.2.4 Emergence of Hotel Services

The hotel or hotel industry has offered clients both nourishing meals and safe accommodation since the beginning of time. Food, clothes, and shelter are the three basic necessities of every human being. The Hotel Industry, for example, provides two basic services:

Food and shelter provisions (accommodation). In ancient times, pilgrims were provided with a variety of amenities in the form of Dharmashalas to allow them to stay at pilgrimage centres. Pilgrims have been offered these dharmashalas' facilities for free or at a low cost by local benefactors or temple officials. These services had been provided by many of the universe's sects. Visitors to the society were served by cathedrals, Buddhist monasteries, and churches. Taverns and inns sprung up all over the place and prospered until the Roman Empire fell apart. Inns were unable to grow due to the rare exchanges of travellers. The crusades laid the foundation for societal reform in Europe. This laid a firm platform for the trade industry's development. Innkeeping has been increasingly popular over time.

People are engaged and well-compensated for their efforts. The first tavern in the United States was established in 1634. The "Hotel" industry was born in these pubs. "A place where guests remained for the night and paid for their meals," the word "hotel" had come to denote. Following then, hotels established a variety of service standards and developed into a separate industry. It is a unique situation in which all of their requirements have been addressed and they are able/willing to provide for their shelter, entertainment, food, and other necessities, according to common law. It was basically a place for the bars to stay temporarily, with all of the facilities and utilities accessible for a price.

The hotel sector is thus designated as a hospitality industry. A hotel, as everyone knows, is a place where clients may relax and pay predetermined costs. They may stay for any number of days and pay for extra amenities such as delicious meals, a private setting, entertainment, sports equipment, sightseeing, and so on. Modern philosophy revolves around the "giving" and "taking" relationships. Hospitality began to expand as a sector as we formalised the word and accepted it as a tool of profit-generating. To put it another way, the hotel business has increased in complexity and played an essential role as a leisure industry.

The 26 firms that gain from this include airlines, cruise ships, buses, and railroads. Furthermore, it has been observed that travel brokers and tour operators are striving for technological excellence. Regulation, technology, and customer expectations are all changing in the hotel business, as they are in many other industries. In 1991, leading chains began entering the Indian market through joint ventures and franchising. Increased competition is one of the most noticeable changes in the Indian hotel business. Consumers now have access to a greater selection of culinary options and services thanks to the arrival of international businesses in India. Consumers are becoming more educated and aware of issues that affect them. The amount of money spent on leisure activities has increased. There's also a perilous mix of business and pleasure travel. In metro centres, too many hotels are being built at a rapid pace, leading demand to surpass supply. In places like Mumbai, Delhi, Chennai, and Khajuraho, the current ability is squeezing the accommodation market. Several new programmes in the nation have been postponed or cancelled due to a funding deficit. The main source of the cash flow problem is that investors are wary of major hotel investments due to worries about increased availability; meanwhile, excellent mid-priced hotels are scarce in smaller locations. Oberois established Trident as a dominant brand in India's mid-sized market. The impact of the seasons on the number of people who visit.

The entire figure was 51 per cent in September and 63.9 per cent in December. On a daily basis, the per centage ranges from 49.1% on Sunday to 59.9% on Thursday. Despite spending less on management and franchise fees, independent hotels' net earnings as a proportion of sales were lower than chain hotels'. Indian hotels have always focused on rooms. At the Taj party, the F&B to Room ratio is 35:65. In New Delhi and Mumbai, the Oberoi properties have a comparable per centage. Room sales, which account for 56.4 per cent of total income across all hotels, are the most crucial source of profit for a hotel. The need for low-cost hotels is increasing in India. The Taj luxury brand is managed in India by Indian Hotels Co. Ltd. The hospitality industry's business leader has entered the budget hotel area through an associate. They opened a sophisticated budget hotel in July 2004 that caters mostly to business travellers. The first hotel has opened in Bangalore's White Field neighbourhood.

1.2.5 Hotel Services

According to new emerging trends in the hotel business, the hotel sector functions as a pool where foreign direct investments flow. The hotel management and domestic tourism of the nation are receiving a lot of attention as a result of the current trends in this industry.

1.2.6 Employment Generation in India

In India, the hospitality sector employs around 41.8 million people. In 2008, hotels and other lodgings employed 1.9 million people. According to the World Travel and Tourism Council, India's tourism sector can sustain 25 million employment by 2012. According to Ma Foi Management Consultants' research, the hotel industry is predicted to generate over 400,000 employments. According to Tourism India, the hotel industry provides 48 million employments in India, either directly or indirectly. This industry employs 8.27 per cent of the workforce. It is expected that for every hotel room built, 3-5 jobs were produced for the workforce. According to the WTTC, India's tourism sector is predicted to increase at an annual rate of 8% by 2014. In September 2014, the number of food services and drinking establishments increased by 20000. Over the course of the year, this industry added around 290000 payroll positions.

1.2.7 Tourism and Hospitality Industry Growth and Development

Furthermore, the government's tourism strategy intends to accelerate the execution of tourist programmes, as well as the development of integrated tourism circuits, unique hospitality sector capacity building, and current marketing tactics and regulations. In India, the tourism and hospitality sector has grown to become one of the country's most vital service providers. Tourism is a substantial sector in India and a major source of foreign income. In addition to being a profitable company, it usually benefits local residents and cultures. In 2013, the industry contributed Rs 2.17 trillion (US$ 36 billion) to the country's overall GDP, accounting for 2% of the country's total GDP (GDP). It is predicted to grow to Rs 4.35 trillion (US$ 72.17 billion) by 2024.

The Indian tourism sector is growing as a result of an increase in foreign tourist arrivals (FTA) and an increase in the number of Indians visiting domestic tourist destinations. According to the WTTC, "the income collected from domestic tourism is anticipated to rise by 8.2 per cent in 2014, compared to 5.1 per cent a year before." Hotels are frequently found in the tourist sector, and they are quite important. The hotel industry in India has been consistently growing at a rate of 14% per year, adding significantly to the country's foreign exchange reserves.

By establishing favourable laws and providing infrastructure help, such as visa simplification and tax breaks for hotels, the Indian government is making a substantial contribution to the industry's growth

1.2.7.1 Hospitality Market

It is a very large market that includes all people who have been in hotels or plan to stay in hotels, as well as all other forms of lodging and restaurants. As a result, the hospitality market encompasses all travellers, tourists, visitors, pilgrims, and others. Depending on the objective of people's journey, they will be categorised into different types of hospitality, such as commercial or leisure.

1.2.7.2 Market Size of the Industry

India's travel and tourism industry is valued at US$ 117.7 billion, with a prediction of US$ 418.9 billion by 2022. In January–March 2014, foreign exchange earnings (FEE) are estimated to be Rs 32,809 crore (US$ 5.44 billion), up 8.4 percent over 2013. 3,883 visa VOAs were issued during this time period, compared to 3,637 VOAs during the same time period in 2013.

1.2.7.3 Foreign Direct Investments

According to data given by the Department of Industry Policy and Promotion, foreign direct investment (FDI) inflows into the hotel and tourist sector totalled US$ 7,013.29 million from April 2000 to January 2014. (DIPP). A few important investments and innovations in the Indian tourist and hospitality business are as follows:

• Hilton Worldwide and Palm Grove Beach Hotels Pvt Ltd, the hospitality arm of the K Raheja Constructions Group, ink a management agreement to open India's first Conrad hotel. Conrad is a Hilton Worldwide premium hotel brand that will open in Pune, Maharashtra, in the future year.

• Lemon Tree Hotels, an Indian hotel chain, is looking to penetrate the premium section of the Indian market. In the United States and Asia, the business is in talks with two luxury labels. Lemon Tree is looking to expand through acquisitions.

• Thomas Cook India and Sterling Holidays have announced a part-cash, part-equity merger to create India's largest vacation provider. According to Mr Ramesh Ramanathan, Managing Director (MD), Sterling Holidays, "the combination intends to develop a vacation behemoth that would take holidays to a bigger audience."

• By 2015, Marriott International intends to open a dozen new hotels in India. The total number of Marriott Hotels in India will now be 23. "We currently have around six to eight confirmed opportunities in 2014, and 2015 is going to be a very good year for us," Rajeev Menon, Area Vice President For South Asia and Australia, adds.

- Muthoot Leisure and Hospitality Services, the Muthoot Group's hospitality branch, has announced the acquisition of Xandari Resort & Spa, Costa Rica's high-end hotel. It is the first purchase in Central America by an Indian hospitality enterprise.

1.2.7.4 Government Initiatives for Hospitality Industry

Clean in India is a campaign initiated by India's Ministry of Tourism to raise awareness about the need of cleanliness and hygiene in public spaces, especially monuments and tourist attractions. It got Rs 4,090.31 crore (US$ 678.54 million) for 1,226 tourist initiatives, including infrastructure upgrades. The government is investigating options for implementing an electronic visa service later this year to liberalise the visa process and put India on the tourism map.

1.2.8 Role of Hotel Management Courses in Hospitality sector

In the hotel and tourist industry, India has a lot of room for growth. Hotel management courses are inextricably tied to the growth of the hotel business. This industry has a significant need for labour, and workforce requirements are increasing by the day. For many departments such as food and beverage, account and finance, food production, housekeeping front office, and many more, hotels require specialised, efficient, and trained personnel. In the current situation, these occupations have gotten more difficult and complicated.

The amount of labour required varies in every hotel and is determined by the hotel's size. By 2001, the hotel business will require more human resources to meet the expansion of room capacity, which is expected to be 124,000 rooms. In a five-star hotel, each room requires three staff members who are responsible for it, with many additional staff members indirectly involved and assisting them.

The majority of hotel employees experience pleasant and comfortable working circumstances. The office crew uses an automated computerised office system that offers the finest working circumstances. Because hotels are open 24 hours a day, personnel work in shifts, which is dependent on a good communication system. The position necessitates a persistent personal appeal, which may be difficult to achieve with customers. This industry provides several career prospects for young men and women with a charming demeanour and a flare for the glamorous world, but it is also a difficult and demanding task. These obstacles can be met by an extrovert with a lively personality. And hotel management courses assist in training the next generation to fulfil all of the industry's demands.

1.2.9 Role of the Multinational Companies

The hotel business plays an important part in the Indian economy's continued expansion. The hotel industry makes a considerable contribution to the economy. The features of services are reflected in the expansion of the service industry. The service deeds, processes, and performance cannot be touched or seen since they are intangible in nature, but they may be felt by the experienced. Because of its diversity, the service industry is a dynamic environment. Because of India's growing service industry, global prospects are expanding. Foreign direct investment has increased India's economic growth as a result of global opportunities. The two most important crucial criteria in determining profitability in this business are occupancy and average room rate. ARR is determined by brand image, goodwill, location, star rating, service quality, facilities, room availability, value-added service price, and other supplementary services. The ARR of hotels is heavily influenced by the season.

1.3 Introduction to Recruitment and Career Advancement:

The recruiting process offers the organisation with a pool of potentially qualified job candidates from which to pick qualified people for hire. The tactics a firm is ready to use in order to find and choose the best applicants have also been tied to the hiring process' efficiency. Organizations seeking entry-level employees often require a minimal set of skills and experience.

The process of gathering a pool of competent individuals and selecting the finest from among them is known as recruitment. High-performing businesses have invested a lot of time and money into developing high-quality selection methods. Human resource management methods, such as recruiting and selection, are critical in determining an organization's performance.

A human resource information system (HRIS) is a technology that collects, stores, manipulates, and analyses data on a person or organisation. It's normal in today's workplace to think about reorganising the old recruiting and selection process using correct decision-making processes. This can improve the quality of recruiting decisions while also increasing the efficacy and efficiency of the procedures.

Data on an organization's human resources is analysed, retrieved, and distributed. The purpose of the system is to help human resource services at all levels, from strategic to tactical to operational. Recruiting and selection are just two of the many decision-making concerns covered. The system promotes the use of automated or computerised techniques to address issues, and it is a critical tool in the information era. Effective recruiting methods and rules, according to researchers, help boards to discover the greatest candidate for their firm. When it comes to recruiting and choosing new administrators, the personnel function is very crucial. When considering administrative responsibilities, one of the most important duties of human resource management is to evoke favourable responses from candidates. When workers are offered possibilities to further their careers in administration (i.e., tapping the shoulders of possible candidates), they frequently react negatively. People who have never worked in an administrative position have poor judgments about the function of the administrator. It is vital to understand what hurdles impede potential candidates from applying to the pool in order to recruit and assist them for the administrator's post. Employees believe that job complexity and workload are the two factors that have had the biggest influence on the number of candidates for administrative positions. Poor compensation in relation to the duties and expectations of the work, as well as a lack of resources and support mechanisms, are further causes. Because they do not want to stay in an office all day, many highly qualified, competent, and brilliant workers decline employment in administration. The problem of pre-screening and identification will not likely improve unless some other image is grasped, or at the very least some assistance and resources are put in place **(Mullins, 1999)**.

1.3.1 Concept of Recruitment:

Employee recruitment is defined by **(Barber, 1998)** as "practises and actions carried out by an organisation to discover and recruit potential personnel." Many major organisations have employee recruiting programmes in place to attract potential workers who will not only fill open jobs but also contribute to the company's culture. **(Costello, 2006)** defines recruitment as "the collection of actions and processes used to lawfully secure a sufficient number of eligible individuals at the proper place and time, so that people and organisations can choose each other in their own best immediate and long-term interests."

1.3.2 Concept of Career:

According to **(Selmer, 1999)**, a career is "a series of related job experiences and tasks, directed at personal and organisational objectives, that an individual passes through throughout his or her lifetime, that are partly under their control and partly under the control of others".

The National Career Development Organization explained in his Guidelines of a federal initiative that combines the hard work of many government departments and professional societies that a career is essentially defined as a path or a route to be travelled, but over time it has come to imply a course of achievement within a field. A career referred to a skilled activity that paid well and had a respectable role and rank with which one could advance during the first seventy-five years of the twentieth century; some people thought of it as "careers," while others thought of it as "employment." The term "career" has come to mean "employment, leisure, and other aspects of one's existence" in the last quarter of the twentieth century.

The Oxford English Dictionary defines a career as "a person's course or growth in life." A person's career is a developmental and lifetime phase that encompasses a wide range of occupational, personal, civic, and political roles that they can fill as adults. Paying jobs, self-employment, unpaid labour, different forms of jobbing, entrepreneurship, home-based businesses, adult education, and unemployment are all included.

1.3.3 Growth & Development of the Concept of Career:

(Geber, 1992) found four unique career reasons. A career can be defined as a route to advancement, an occupation, a lifelong series of occupations, or a lifelong sequence of role-related events, to name a few examples.

- **A career as a means of advancement**

A profession can refer to vertical or upward advancement within an organisation. A promotion, a move, or a new job in a higher function in a different organisation are all examples of how an individual develops in their professional career. It might also imply a lateral movement with increasing responsibilities. A profession correlates to easy development in this sense, such as a sales agent rising through the sales department's ranks to become a sales manager **(Geber, 1992)**.

- **A profession is a job that you do for a living**.

This concept pertains to vocations in which an individual is obligated to follow a certain path throughout their career; in other words, there is a clear progression pattern. A lawyer is an excellent example of such a profession. An individual begins as a law student, proceeds to a law firm clerk after finishing his or her papers, then to an associate, and lastly to a partner after earning sufficient experience or skill **(Geber, 1992)**.

- **A career is a set of roles that you play throughout the course of your life**.

This is a word that refers to a collection of occupations that a person has held during the course of their career. There is no mention of a specific occupation or mobility; rather, it applies to any job held by the worker during the course of his or her career **(Geber, 1 992)**.

- **A job might be viewed as a lifetime of role-related interactions**.

This is the process through which a person rotates work functions and acquires expertise. It's similar to a psychological experience (pleasure, objectives moving, and attitudes shifting **(Geber, 1992)**.

In general, a profession is a series of tasks that individuals may rise through a hierarchy of positions in order to earn power, prestige, and rewards. It refers to a technical or administrative role in this context. Various scholars, on the other hand, have presented a variety of profession descriptions, many of which varied greatly between fields.

According to **(Arthur et al., 1989)**, the term "career" in academic science has a far broader connotation. It is not limited to practitioners and may apply to everyone who works. Various disciplines, including psychology, sociology, anthropology, economics, political science, history, and geography, have recognised different notions of occupation. In political science, for example, a career is defined as "the study of individuals' quests for power, money, and social status within a political framework." It reflects on the labour market, people's creation of human resources, and job prospects in the field of economics.

It focuses on how the distribution of geographical resources affects work in the geography field. It originally emerged in the memoirs of famous persons who were involved in historical events. History and community are two career paths in anthropology. The intermediating roles and relationships between social systems and individuals are the subject of sociology theory.

According to **(Richardson, 1993 and Super, 1980)**, the term "career" encompasses all people who serve outside of organisations, such as housewives, and it may also refer to duties that deal with time processes, according to Barley.

Career studies have a long history in sociology, extending back to **(Barley's, 1989)** research in the Chicago school, which focused on deviant behaviour and life records. The term "career" is used by sociologists to describe something that has to do with one's life path, such as a criminal career, a medical career, or a family career. Life-course research, according to Elder, has recently maintained this trend.

In his research, **(Marshall, 1989)** presented the feminist view of the profession. It was identified in the feminist viewpoint, which previously focused mostly on cultural preconceptions and factors that prevented women from receiving equal pay as men. According to feminist opinions, career is now more women-centred, stressing women's own aspirations and cherishing their dedication to marriages and families rather than perceiving them as setbacks from men's perspectives.

According to **(Shartle, 1959)** and **(Super, 1980)** in vocational psychology, a career was formerly defined as the advancement of authority or duty along the occupational system's hierarchy. As vocational behaviour became recognised as a vital aspect of an individual's whole existence, the concept of profession emerged. A career, for example, is defined as "the mix and sequence of responsibilities done by an individual during a lifetime."

(Arnold, 2001) used a similarly broad definition, describing a career as "a succession of employment-related jobs, duties, activities, and experiences undertaken by an individual."

In industrial sociology, the study of sequences of professions gave rise to the concept of a profession. This term was largely used in the workplace to describe the number, size, and sequences/hierarchies of positions. According to the sociology field, career patterns tend to be utilised to demonstrate professional adaptability. Following a comprehensive examination of the research and full comprehension of the tradition, it was revealed that professional vocations are separated into three phases: orderliness (order/disorder), direction (vertical/horizontal), and continuity (stable/changing). However, this difference is not strictly adhered to by all organisations. For example, **(Miller and Form, 1951)** observed that consistency may frequently be used to explain why people maintain the same level of work. When it comes to women's vocations, however, the concept of a work pattern is later enlarged to include non-working periods.

1.3.4   Career Path

"Career path" is described by **(Rao and Rao, 1990)** as "the sequential pattern of occupations that creates a career."

"Career path" is defined by **(Prasad, 2005)** as "the logical conceivable sequence of roles that an individual might have based on how he performs in the organisation." A career path is made up of two parts: a line and a ladder. Production, marketing, finance, HRM, and other fields of specialisation are examples of lines. There are several positions placed in hierarchical order inside each line. When someone is placed on a career path, it shows how they will advance to those roles. The alignment of individual requirements, talents and limitations, and organisational opportunities determines this placement.

1.3.5 Progression In the Career

(Judge et al., 1995) defined "career success" as "individual extrinsic/objective and intrinsic/subjective accomplishments in their professional lives." Careers are assessed in intrinsic terms using personal subjective perceptions of success or failure, rather than in external ones using external reference points or standards, according to **(Gattiker and Larwood, 1988)**.

According to studies, unlike extrinsic professional achievement, intrinsic career success is mostly driven by personality, with no consistent impacts of general mental ability and very little experience effects **(Bozionelos, 2004)**. There is, however, a link between intrinsic work enjoyment (work happiness) and expansive professional success (pay, promotions, and job level) that has been proved in various studies as indicated by **(Judge et al., 2004)**.

"Career progress is defined as the accumulated good work and psychological results coming from one's job experiences," according to **(Seibert and Kraimer, 2001)**. "Career progression is frequently described in terms of promotion within managerial ranks," writes **(Naidoo, 2004)**. "Good psychological or job-related outcomes or achievements are that an individual acquires as a result of work experiences," says Seibert.

Term career progression is frequently operationalized in one of two ways by researchers:

- The first method, according to **(Gutteridge, 1973) and (Judge et al., 1995)**, comprises variables that assess objective or extrinsic career advancement. These markers of job development include pay achievement and the number of promotions in one's career, both of which can be seen and thus objectively judged by others.

- According to **(Judge et al., 1995)** and **(Burke, 2001)**, the second technique to operationalize career development is through variables that assess subjective or intrinsic career advancement. Individuals' subjective evaluations regarding their work accomplishments, such as job and career satisfaction, are captured by such variables.

1.3.6 Obstacles To Career Progression

Professional obstacles are described by **(Swanson and Woitke, 1997)** and **(Smith, 2004)** as "events or factors, either inside the person or in his or her environment, that make career advancement difficult." Career growth might be difficult due to increased credentials and economic changes, as well as internal (psychological) and external (environmental) interferences. Career progression hurdles, according to **(Mc Whirter, 1997)**, explain the persistent ability and achievement difference in people's vocational choices. The following are some of the possible professional growth roadblocks:

- **Dual career families**

Rao and Rao (1990) discovered that in a dual-career family, one of the members may have difficulty advancing in their job owing to a spouse's move, overwork, or other factors. The conflict between work and family duties, as well as a desire to spend more time with family, were shown to be the most prevalent hurdles to women's professional progression (Campbell, 1999). Regardless of their work level, Indian women continue to carry the weight of domestic tasks, according to **(Bharat, 1992)** and **(Ramu, 1989).** For familial considerations, Indian women, according to **(Desai, 1996)**, prefer to limit their job objectives or personal achievements.

- **Career with a low ceiling**

Despite a decent career plan and progress, **(Rao and Rao, 1990)** discovered that certain jobs do not have much room for advancement.

- **Inadequate career counselling**

According to **(Rao and Rao, 1990)**, certain career development activities may be hindered by a lack of career counselling and a lack of training and education programmes for younger managers.

- **Organizational structure that is flat**

According to **(Rao and Rao, 1990)**, organisations that have a flat organisational structure may limit opportunities for advancement.

- **Ethnic considerations**

Ethnic minorities, according to **(Smith, 2004)**, report more impediments to find work, job performance, and career balance than non-minorities.

1.3.7 Strategies For Advancing Your Career

Individuals and organisations must respond strategically to perceived hurdles to development in their careers. The following are some possible ways for getting through professional growth roadblocks:

- Education helps people to understand their own strengths, requirements, and motivations, according to (Rao and Rao, 1990). Providing proper educational facilities, commencing career counselling, and creating more flexible incentive and promotion systems are just a few examples of what might be done.
- • Taking greater personal responsibility for one's professional development appears to be a common trend among professionals, according to research (Craig, 1998). It was also found that networking is employed as a means of advancing one's career. The importance of establishing a professional network cannot be overstated. Recruiters and placement specialists agree that building a professional network should be part of any long-term career strategy. It's critical to keep those who aren't affiliated with the present institutions informed. Moving people laterally and assisting employees in finding new challenges in their present roles are becoming more

commonly recognised career development options, according to the research. Volunteering one's expertise for any tasks that might lead to the desired employment.

- **(Campbell, 1999)** discovered that making it easy for employees to shift jobs had a positive impact. Accepting increasing job responsibilities or new tasks, shifting to a different department or service, and changing professions that required learning new skills were all factors that helped people advance in their careers. Supportive measures were employed since there were positive correlations between the wide range of career boosters and social support.

1.3.8 Career Advancement Theories

It's crucial to understand how managers grow in their careers. For those who are the most effective, there is a need to rise to higher levels.

According to **(Erwee, 1988)**, poor management performance leads to failure, whereas strong management performance leads to profitability. According to **(Kotter, 1996)**, today's organisations have different techniques of advancing to higher positions than they had two decades ago. Career advancement used to be determined by job ladders, seniority, and tenure. However, according to **(Naidoo, 2004)**, there are fewer posts now, the organisation is flat, and there is more decentralisation. Career progression occurs as a result of these changes.

Selection and promotion methods are now more systematic and less subjective than they were a decade ago, according to **(Kotter, 1998)**. Equal employment opportunities, a diversified candidate pool for management jobs, and a greater number of applicants from various ethnic groups and races characterise the current job market.

1.3.8.1 Mobility of the Career

Career mobility is defined by **(Naidoo, 2004)** as "an individual's movement to develop his own career." The two major theoretical approaches on career mobility, according to **(Tumer, 1960)**, are (1) the contest-mobility point of view; (2) the sponsored-mobility point of view.

Upward mobility study is crucial for professional advancement because persons who can move up the social or organisational ladder are generally seen as successful. According to **(Rosenbuam, 1984)** and **(Wayne et al., 1999)**, a contest-mobility system displays the core principle that all persons can struggle for upward mobility. Although two points of view are essentially opposed, they are not mutually exclusive. A society or an institution may have an upward mobility system that favours one perspective over the other.

- **Viewpoint on contest mobility**

According to Becker, success on the job and creating value for the business are the most important factors in moving forward in an organisation **(Becker, 1964)**. Only one's own ability and performance may catapult one to the next level. Human capital is highly valued in the labour market and should be considered when predicting career progression. Human capital factors include hours worked, job centrality, employment longevity, organisation tenure, work experience, and willingness.

- **Perspective on sponsored mobility**

According to the sponsored-mobility concept, persons in positions of power (established elites) pay special attention to personnel with great potential and subsequently give sponsorship activities to assist them in winning the race.

People who succeed early in their careers are more likely to be sponsored, whereas those who do not are frequently barred from such opportunities. Organizational sponsorship is determined by a variety of factors, including career sponsorship, supervisor support, training and skill development opportunities, and organisational resources. They are given preferential treatment to help them grow even better once they have been identified as potential elites, and they are even isolated from the perhaps non-elite group. This indicates, in a figurative sense, that future elites will start the race sooner, gain momentum faster, and win more medals and championships. According to **(Kanter, 1977)**, socio-demographic variables like gender and race are frequently employed as a criterion for allocating sponsorship. Employers allocate individual women to lower-level positions, according to **(Tharenou, 1997)** and **(Greenhaus et al., 1990)**. In comparison to Whites, non-Whites may be perceived as less capable and unworthy of organisational support.

Married people may be given sponsorship, according to **(Pfeffer and Ross, 1982)**, since they are more stable and responsible than unmarried people. Finally, according to **(Ng et al. 2005)**, sponsorship tasks may be disproportionately given to those who are more talented and experienced, because both experience and organisational knowledge grow with age. Using these two views, the researchers discovered four sets of factors that are widely cited as predictors of professional success. Human capital, organisational sponsorship, socio-demographic status, and consistent individual differences are all factors. They claim that the competitive mobility lens has historically been utilised to assess career achievement using human capital determinants (such as job experience or expertise). Human capital, according to **(Becker, 1964) and (Wayne et al. 1999),** refers to an individual's educational, personal, and professional experiences that might help them succeed in their careers. It is frequently used as a predictor of job success.

Some of the characteristics that determine a person's human capital include the amount of hours worked, work centrality (i.e. job participation), job tenure, organisation tenure, and foreign work experience. The number and/or quality of established contacts, known as social capital, is a significant part of political knowledge and abilities, identified by **(Ng et al. 2005)**.

Similarly, the sponsored-mobility paradigm has traditionally employed organisational sponsorship and socio-demographic status to assess career achievement.

Individual differences were not included in **(Turner's, 1960)** model, and they do not appear to be more closely associated with one perspective than the other. And **(Ng et al. 2005)** included stable individual difference factors since they have often been explored in earlier studies on a career. Extroversion, proactivity, internal locus of control and cognitive ability are all stable individual difference characteristics. True, the sponsored system simply provides managers with a shortcut approach for swiftly identifying their emerging stars. This strategy is excellent for any company in its early stages of development or a labour-shortage situation.

On the other hand, the sponsored system has at least two weaknesses. The danger of selection mistakes is the first problem uncovered by **(Rosenbaum, 1984)**. When competent individuals are wrongly dismissed early in their careers, they will have limited opportunity to exhibit their qualities later. Employees who are aware that they are being considered for top jobs do not have to contemplate the long-term consequences of their behaviour.

The second disadvantage discovered by **(Wailerdsak and Suehiro, 2004)** is that if potential managers are recognised early in their career paths, the motivation of those who are not, which is a much bigger group, is likely to drop. Non-selected personnel are not guaranteed more possibilities for growth, no matter how hard they work. This may result in less efficient utilisation of human resources overall. As a result, the sponsored system appears to be improper for a well-known, respected corporation with a pool of well-trained staff.

1.3.8.2 Career Advancement: Objective Vs. Subjective

Career success has been regarded mostly from the standpoint of the individual employee by researchers. Although there are studies that employ both objective and subjective judgments, empirical research on professional success undertaken by **(Greenhaus, 2003)** and **(Poole and Langan-Fox, 1993)** has tended to use objective metrics. Total remuneration, for example, is an objective metric of professional success. A specified number of promotions and other achievements must be demonstrated. Subjective career advancement focuses on intangible factors such as job satisfaction and recognition, whereas objective career advancement states that people who earn higher salaries and are promoted faster are typically regarded as more successful in their careers, whereas objective career advancement states that people who earn higher salaries and are promoted faster are typically regarded as more successful in their careers, and so on, according to **(Judge et al. 1995)**. Career advances are linked both objectively and subjectively. Objective professional growth (concrete career successes) may eventually lead to better job happiness (intangible career achievements). Getting a greater income and more promotions than others will undoubtedly improve one's perceptions of advancement. In a culture where wealth and social status are valued, concrete career accomplishments may contribute to emotions of increased job satisfaction. It's worth noting that objective professional development isn't always a good indication of subjective career growth.

Certain socio-demographic groups endure pay and promotion discrimination, according to **(Greenhaus et al. 1990)**. Personality is linked to perceptual characteristics such as Subjective professional growth, according to **(Bell and Staw, 1989)**. Organizational sponsorship, according to **(Salancik and Pfeffer, 1978)**, is likely to result in better levels of job satisfaction and a stronger feeling of professional development. According to **(Ng et al. 2005)**, the human capital component is a better predictor of objective career development than subjective career advancement.

Employees with a high degree of education who worked in larger businesses with well-structured progression ladders and devoted significant effort in their job function reported the highest objective career success, according to **(Nabi, 1999)**. Employees with a high job centrality score worked in organisations with well-structured advancement ladders and employment security, and networked often despite a lack of desire, and rated the greatest subjective career success.

1.3.9 Career Advancement:

Professional development is a learning process in which generic competence abilities are acquired and used to make career decisions, carry them out, and achieve job and life happiness. Career development is the continuous, continuous process of developing and implementing a self-idea, assessing it against reality, and achieving self-satisfaction and society benefit described by **(Super, 1957)**. In the late 1980s, the National Career Development Guidelines integrated many of the concepts proposed by career development pioneers. Career development is defined in these principles as a lifelong process of learning about ourselves in connection to the workplace.

Career development, according to **(Simonsen, 1994)**, is a continuous process of planning, action, and achievement of personal work and life goals; growth, continuous acquisition, and application of one's skills; it is the result of an individual's career planning and the organization's provision of support and opportunities, and it is best described as a collaborative process.

Career development, according to **(Cummings and Worley, 2005)**, assists individuals in reaching their professional objectives and consists mostly of a person's career planning and organisational policies that help workers put their plans into action. Techniques include skill training, performance evaluation and mentoring, regular work rotation, mentorship, and continuous education.

In **(Gilley and Eggland, 2002)** career development was defined as a collaborative effort that brings together individuals and businesses to build a partnership that enhances employees' understanding, abilities, competencies, and mindsets for current and future job responsibilities. It is a must-do development activity since enhanced personal performance contributes to the success of the company.

1.3.10 Career Advancement/Development Required:

Career advancement is highly important or necessary for an individual's and an organization's considerable progress. It has a significant influence and benefits both parties.

Both the individual and the company are affected. According to (**Jackson Jr. and Sirianni, 2009)**, an organization's sustainability is solely dependent on its human capital, and it seeks to make better use and growth of its talent, which necessitates a bigger investment in its career development. Improved efficiency, profitability, company growth, and maybe even survival will be achieved as a result of this investment. Employees who participate in important career development programmes are more likely to be satisfied with their jobs and loyal to their employers, resulting in lower employee turnover. As a result, higher consumer satisfaction and company productivity result. High employee turnover in service organisations such as banks and investment entities, hospitals, hotels, and tourism, according to **(Brox, 2007)**, causes buyers to question whether their money is safe because new people are constantly changing, and every new image behind the teller line is a new face for buyers to get to know and trust. Employers that can no longer promise permanent employment or advancement in their careers are increasingly relying on employee development programmes to retain and motivate their workers. With the objective of increasing employee success and loyalty to the company's goals, career growth is now less blatantly addressed and more focus is placed on personal development.

Individual benefits, according to **(Ball, 1998)**, include a better level of "marketability" both inside the organisation and in the external labour market, as well as a stronger sense of fulfilment and job satisfaction. Career planning and development provides insight and direction for individual employees, as well as a means of dealing with ambiguous role requirements and organisational demands, identifying career opportunities, reducing stress associated with career changes, and empowering opportunities such as coaching and training.

Employees are given the opportunity to develop their skills and knowledge of how to perform a wide range of tasks in order to improve their performance and efficiency. (Selmer, 1999) stated that development empowers employees by delegating decision-making authority down the organisational hierarchy and allowing lower-level employees to gain additional responsibilities. Career management may address the developing spiritual needs of employees in order to increase their work and life happiness. According to **(Ma and Ma, 2006)**, career management increases self-satisfaction with work, makes work more meaningful, and life more pleasant, and helps people to be more future-oriented.

Career development therapies, according to Savickas, significantly simplify occupational choice and increase job adjustment by assisting individuals in gaining self-awareness about where they may be fulfilled and satisfied. Because today's economy necessitates the ability to switch jobs on a regular basis, the interventions assist job changers in determining which positions are the easiest for them to move into and the exact skills they need to obtain in order to make smooth job transitions.

1.4 Career Development Approaches

1.4.1 Organizational Strategy

- **The traditional idea of a job**

Many companies have well-established career advancement tracks for people viewed as having promise, with the expectation of continuous lifelong service within the company. Much of the typical career planning technique appears to be based on the premise that one works for a major corporation. It is in this setting that planned career pathways or routes might be identified. The conventional method to career development has a number of distinguishing characteristics including hierarchies and classifications that allow for skill advancement and growth.

(Super, 1957) pioneered the typical career paradigm, which emphasises extrinsic incentives and organisational career management in a linear and upward career progression across one or two enterprises.

People who follow a traditional career path are more likely to have been with their employer for 10 years or more, and to move between different companies. Age, organisational or workforce service time are widely employed as proxies for career stage, such as the Super's trademarked career concerns assessment. The old concept of organisational career development, according to **(McDonald and Hite, 2005)**, was based on the idea of building a career inside an organisation and having predictable, steady work.

Traditionally, career planning and management involved setting a trajectory within an organisational structure that would result in promotions or increases in responsibility as knowledge evolved, and then sticking to it. Regularly planned training programmes, work rotation, and maybe some types of informal mentorship were frequently used to achieve professional goals.

- **The idea of a career in a tournament:**

According to **(Rosenbaum, 1984)** and **(Walton, 1999)**, a number of firms appear to use a 'tournament' model of career development for employees seeking managerial advancement as their career anchors, in which early tournament performance is considered as a predictor of subsequent growth. In fact, in order to stay in the game, an employee must win in the early rounds. Until people reach their early thirties, they must go through years of training, job rotation, and general socialising. Those perceived to have great potential are then promoted faster than the rest of their classmates, who may be pushed to quit. Even if it isn't coupled with such a precise strategy, the concept of a tournament is a potent metaphor. When promotion possibilities are few – as they are in delayered and shrunk companies – competition for positions can become fierce. Of course, this implies that vertical advancement and hierarchical rank remain as goals to be pursued, an assumption rooted in the conventional idea of a career.

- "Contemporary career" as a personal approach:

According to **(Sullivan and Baruch, 2009)**, in the early to mid-1990s, a greater emphasis was placed on jobs outside of organisations. Employees who had placed their career goals on progress inside a specific business came to learn that the future of their careers rested on their own initiative as things changed; career planning took on a new dimension as organisations shrunk, right-sized, and restructured. According to **(McDonald and Hite, 2005)** a new career vocabulary emerged, redefining commonly used terms such as career and job to incorporate a broader perspective. As a result, according to **(Arthur and Rousseau, 1996)**, a person's career broadened to encompass not just their place and kind of occupation, but also their employability through time, and employment became more than simply a tool to describe "hierarchical growth." There are three major shifts in the transition from organization-based to multidivisional careers, **(Forret and Sullivan, 2002)** note. One shift from interest in high salaries and work status to objectives outlined by individual interests and work-life harmony. The second note a shift from developing organization-specific skill sets to acquiring transferable skills that can move with the individual.

• Protean profession:

(Halls, 1996b) proposed the protean career theory, which stresses that individual professional growth is their responsibility. According to **(Sullivan and Baruch, 2009)**, the protean careerist can rearrange and repackage his or her knowledge, skills, and abilities to meet the demands of a changing workplace as well as his or her need for self-fulfilment, using the metaphor of the Greek god Proteus, who could change his shape at will. Career management and growth are in the hands of the person, not the business. The protean career, according to **(Lopes, 2006)**, is a career development perspective in which the individual, rather than the employer, is in charge of his or her career management, growth, and decisions. The essential values for deciding success in a multifaceted job are a high amount of freedom, autonomy, and flexibility.

Subjective success, such as psychological success, vs objective success, which includes both position and money, are the key success criterion. Protean career, according to **(Hall, 1996)**, captures the individual character of professional advancement, which is driven by the individual and evolutionary in nature, rather than fostered by and connected to an organisation. Protean career, according to **(Carbery and Garavan, 2007)**, focuses on the subjective perspective of the individual career actor, and it assumes that the individual will drive his or her career and establish goals that span the whole living space.

Individuals with volatile career attitudes, according to **(Briscoe, Hall, and DeMuth, 2005)**, are committed to utilising their own beliefs (rather than company norms, for example) to govern their careers ("values-driven") and taking control of their professional behaviour ("self-directed"). Individuals without protean attitudes are more prone to "steal" external norms rather than create their own, and to seek professional direction and help in cognitive career planning rather than being aggressive and self-sufficient.

(Briscoe and Hall,2006) stated that, while most protean have a greater level of flexibility and a learning attitude, these characteristics are not needed for a protean career. Briscoe and Hall redefined the entrepreneurial attitude concept by defining two dimensions: (1) values-driven in the sense that internal values guide and measure career success; and (2) self-directed in personal career management.

- **Career Management Process:**

According to **(Armstrong, 2001)**, Career management is the process of transitioning from one stage of your career to another. The goal of career management is to: a)

Meet the demands of the organization's management succession. b) Provide a training and experience programme for promising men and women that will prepare them for whatever level of responsibility they are capable of. To construct a unified career development process, the researcher used components of **(Jackson Jr, Hollmann, and Gallan's, 2006)** salespersons career development model as well as **(Armstrong's, 2001)** holistic career management strategy.

1.5 Self-Efficacy: An Overview:

According to research, having a strong feeling of personal effectiveness has been linked to improved learning performance **(Guest, 1992b)**. A worker's view that he or she is capable of developing and growing his or her capabilities is characterised as self-efficacy for the growth and enhancement of career-relevant abilities. According to **(Maurer, 2001)**. Individuals with the self-confidence to execute their careers and the self-efficacy to combine their present and former self-efficacy are seen as having the genuine career notion. "Self-efficacy is likely to impact the amount to which a person pursues a protean profession," writes **(Svejenova, 2005)**. **(Maurer, 2001)** The self-efficacy for development construct refers to a person's ability to grow and learn across a variety of possible development/learning activities that they may experience throughout their career. Although there may be disparities in self-efficacy for different developmental activities depending on one's prior experiences and talents, as well as current resources, it focuses on a more general belief in one's ability to learn and improve as needed within one's profession.

People's self-efficacy and desire to exercise control over professional outcomes, according to **(King, 2004)** allow people to participate in career self-management behaviours that can lead to the achievement of desired professional goals and ultimate career success. **(Ballout, 2009)** mentioned that, according to a study conducted by the American Psychological Association (APA) and the US National Institute of Occupational and Related Health Sciences, individuals with a strong feeling of job commitment and self-efficacy are more likely to achieve high levels of career success (NIH). Individuals with high levels of self-efficacy reduced the favourable impacts of professional dedication on both objective and subjective job success, according to the research.

1.5.1 Occupational Attitudes:

"An attitude might roughly be characterised as an established pattern of thinking, it is evaluated," writes **(Armstrong, 2001)**. People form attitudes, but they are less permanent than qualities, and they are prone to change when new experiences or influences are gained. Cultural components (values and conventions), managerial behaviour (management style), and regulations such as salary, recognition, promotion, and work-life quality all have an impact. According to **(Pilbeam and Corbridge, 2002)**, attitudinal flexibility implies an emphasis on encouraging flexible employee attitudes, such as receptivity to acquiring new skills, readiness to engage in functional flexibility, and responsiveness to changes in working practises or management techniques. Through integrated human resource strategies and corporate value management, flexible attitudes and behaviour may be identified, acknowledged, and encouraged.

Super's career maturity model includes two main components: attitudes toward and competencies for creating a profession. Planning attitudes mediate the process of considering and planning for one's professional future. Individuals with mature views are more likely to plan ahead, use a methodical approach, and actively participate in career planning activities. Individuals with immature views are frequently disinclined to look ahead to their future in the workplace; as a result, they do not feel the need to familiarise themselves with or relate to vocations. The willingness to identify and use effective resources for career planning is measured by attitudes toward career exploration. Individuals with immature attitudes toward exploration are frequently careless about accessing reliable sources of information concerning fields and degrees of employment **(Savickas, Briddick and Watkins Jr, 2002)**.

1.5.2 Awareness of Oneself:

(The Oxford advanced learner's dictionary of modern English, published in 1995) Self-awareness is the state of knowing one's own personality, sentiments, and other characteristics. It is the organization's capacity to establish an atmosphere that openly encourages employees to develop self-awareness and to hire people who know exactly what they want from work and the business. According to them **(Young, 2009)**. It may also make recruiting and selection easier, allowing people to be put in organisations and professions where they can contribute. **(Church, 1997)** defines managerial self-awareness as "the capacity to reflect on and accurately analyse one's own behaviours and skills as they show in workplace interactions." Workers' views of development requirements are separated into two categories, according to **(Noe and Wilk, 1993)** understanding of development requirements and level of agreement with the organization's evaluation of those needs. When a learner understands the importance of polishing certain abilities, he or she will be more driven to participate in development activities and, as a result, more dedicated to learning and development.

The learner's ability to effectively appraise his or her own strengths, shortcomings, and work styles will determine how successful training and development interventions are. A stated emphasis on self-improvement is a key component of an organization's career development policy. Increased self-awareness in the learner will lead to more effective self-development. Self-awareness, according to **(Peterson and Hicks, 1995)**, is critical for self-development. Individuals are actively involved in their own professional growth, according to this perspective on work. **(Levinson, 1989)** discusses how to manage one's own professional growth. He claims that self-examination by the learner yields a slew of benefits. Growing individuals, according to **(McCarthy and Garavan, 1999)**, "analyse themselves and emerge with new levels of drive, a clearer sense of direction, and a more vital insight of how they want to live on the job."

1.6 The Hotel's Employees

Staff motivation is a critical problem in the hotel industry since it is linked to employee turnover and overall hotel service quality **(Chen, 2013)**. The degree of service provided to customers determines a hotel's overall profitability. As a result, the hotels' top objective is to motivate its employees so that they can help the hoteliers succeed. To put it another way, job satisfaction is crucial for retaining and inspiring employees to provide and offer superior customer care. As a consequence, the study thesis focuses on the Indian hotel industry in order to explore the factors that positively affect employee performance and can assist hotels in retaining staff for longer periods of time, hence decreasing turnover rates.

1.6.1 Performance of Employees

Because employees are one of the most precious assets, employee performance is one of the most important variables in determining a hotel's profitability. This is because the hospitality industry is a manpower-intensive industry, and hotels must place a priority on employee performance and take steps to enhance it. Furthermore, in the hotel industry, employee performance is crucial since guests interact directly with hotel personnel, and hotel workers are responsible for client satisfaction. Apart from focusing on hotel amenities and services, hoteliers and managers must also be concerned with boosting the elements that might increase staff performance.

1.6.2 Employee Perceptions of Their Work

Employee motivation, contentment, and engagement are important themes in both the practical and theoretical aspects of hotel management **(Costen and Salazar, 2011; DiPietro, Kline and Nierop, 2014; Khalilzadeh, Giacomo, Jafari and Hamid, 2013).** This is the case since workers are an important part of the service delivery process **(Zeithaml, Berry and Parasuraman, 1988).** Although the physical environment, methods, and procedures are important components of service delivery, their success is based on human resources' energy and talents. Because most services cannot be delivered without the presence of human resources, the hotel sector is a labour-intensive enterprise **(Hazra, Sengupta and Ghosh, 2014).** The human factor is what makes it possible to give services. When it comes to providing these services, the hotel industry prioritises motivated, happy, and engaged human resources. Customers' happiness or discontent with the services supplied can be impacted by a variety of factors.

1.7 Problem Statement for Research

According to the World Economic Forum, India placed 10th out of 185 nations in terms of overall contribution to GDP from travel and tourism in 2019. (World Travel and Tourism Council). In 2019, travel and tourism contributed 6.8% of the total economy's GDP, or Rs. 13,68,100 crore (US$ 194.30 billion). The government's relaxation of tourist visa rules and investment in critical infrastructure have enticed investors and global hotel companies. Mumbai, Bengaluru, Pune, Gurugram, and other Indian cities are famous business tourism destinations. It contains 4- and 5-star hotels that provide exceptional service to foreign business travellers.

The ethnically varied work pool at India's hotels makes motivating and satisfying staff even more challenging. With multinational hotel chains increasingly interested in entering the Indian hotel industry, this paper will examine the variables that influence employee perceptions of their jobs, as well as how to inspire, please, and engage hotel employees in India.

1.8 The Study's Purpose

In the Indian setting, only a few studies have looked at hospitality professionals' (including current employees who are working in the industry and students who are studying hospitality) job satisfaction. This study may aid hotel managers in being more aware of their workers' job happiness and engagement levels, as well as what drives them to work. This study adds to previous research by expanding it into a new setting. The following were the objectives of this research:

1. To investigate and study the literature on hotel professionals' job satisfaction, engagement, and motivating variables.
2. To look at the factors that influence hotel professionals' motivation, satisfaction, and engagement in India.
3. Make comments and recommendations to Indian hotel management and academia in order to improve employees' happiness and changes in training needs for students.

1.9 Research Questions

This study analyses work perception levels among hotel employees in India based on these concerns. The research is guided by the following questions:

- Do current hotel employees intend to pursue their careers in the industry?
- What factors do employees find important when considering a career?
- How well do they think the hospitality industry offers these factors?

Have contingency variables (gender, year of study, work experience, and willingness to pursue a particular major) been linked to current perceptions of the industry?

1.10 Significance Of the Study

The conclusions of this study will help top management better comprehend India's varied labour population and give tools to help them manage their human capital. This study's findings will help hotel managers establish better policies and procedures that will improve staff happiness and morale, resulting in great customer service and strong customer loyalty. Furthermore, this research has implications for academia, since it may lead to new discoveries and the development of new curricula and methods for hotel management students.

1.11 Research Objectives

The purpose of this research thesis is to assess the influence of employee perception and extrinsic motivation on service quality in the Indian hotel sector. The inability of employees to perform at their best due to a lack of job satisfaction will result in a reduction in the quality of services provided to consumers, which will have an indirect impact on the industry's profitability. As a result, hotel managers must understand the requirements, perceptions, ambitions, and expectations of their workers while serving clients in order to recruit, retain, and motivate them. The thesis also aims to evaluate the numerous elements that have a direct influence on employees' perceptions. Based on the variables, hotel managers may implement a variety of management techniques and tools to improve employee happiness, which will inspire them to work better.

The following are the key objectives of the research thesis based on the problem statement:

1. Examining the present perceptions of employees towards the hospitality industry as a career choice.
2. To identify the key challenges of employees facing in 5-star hotels in India.
3. To identify the major key factor which affects the employees of 5-star hotels in India
4. Evaluate the impact of major factors on the perception of hotel's employees working in 5-star hotels.
5. Providing a list of specific remedial activities that hospitality stakeholders should take to improve the industry's reputation as a career option.

1.12 Limitation

One of the thesis's limitations is that it solely considers the impact of 5-star hotel professionals' perception on career progression and the elements that influence their performance in the Indian hotel sector. It excludes other factors of the hotel business that might have a detrimental influence on staff performance, such as guest types, customer attitudes, lack of cash available to hoteliers, hotel location, and so on. Another limitation is that it is only focusing hotel's employees and hospitality students' perceptions about careers and does not focus on guests' perceptions and attitudes about the hospitality industry. These factors are not taken into account in the thesis while analysing approaches for improving hospitality professionals' performance in Indian hotels.

1.13 Summary Of the Chapters

The first chapter provides an overview of the thesis topic as well as the reasoning for selecting it as a research thesis topic. In addition to providing a short background on the study issue, the chapter describes the research thesis's goals and objectives. In the final section of the chapter, the research topics and constraints are discussed.

The second chapter contains a study of academic literature and valuable research works in the field of the thesis's subject matter, on which the thesis's research hypotheses are founded.

The thesis' research hypotheses are established in the second chapter, which includes a survey of academic literature and helpful research works in the field of the research topic.

The third chapter discusses research methodology, which comprises the researcher's research methodologies and procedures for collecting and analysing data in order to meet the thesis's goal.

The fourth chapter presented the research findings based on the data, and the last chapter included the study conclusion as well as brief recommendations for further research in the research issue.

CHAPTER – II

2 LITERATURE REVIEW

2.1 Career Decision-Making: A Conceptual Framework

(Krumboltzs, 1979), The social learning theory of professional decision-making is one of the most important contributions to the field of business and management theory. It has contributed in the creation of a conceptual framework for understanding how individuals make professional decisions at various stages in their lives. The next part discusses the basic features and applications of social learning theory of professional decision-making.

The notion of professional decision-making was first proposed in 1909, but it was not until 1979 that the phrase "career decision-making" became widely recognized. In 1909, Frank Parsons was the first to develop the concept of career decision-making. **(Patton and McMahon, 1999),** in his book "Choosing a Vocation," he addressed his thoughts on how careers are chosen. "(1) a thorough awareness of yourself, your talents, interests, aspirations, resources, and limits, as well as the reasons behind these things; (2) in many domains of employment, a comprehension of the demands, success conditions, advantages and drawbacks, compensation, chances, and prospects; according to

These three major components of vocational choice presented easy suggestions for people to consider when deciding on a job, emphasising the necessity of people understanding themselves, their job alternatives, and how to use this data to make sound professional decisions **(Jones, 1994).**

Michael Krumboltz introduced his "social learning theory of professional decision-making" in 1979, and the phrase "career decision-making" was coined for the first time **(Brown, 2002).**

A process that outlines or explains the decisions a person takes while choosing a career may be characterised as career decision-making. It also aids in the identification of many variables that influence a person's professional decisions and choices, as well as a knowledge of how these factors influence their career options and preferences. **(Sharf, 2002).**

Recently, there has been more. advancements in the vocation dynamic speculations. However, Parsons' professional choice hypothesis has remained incredibly persuasive, and his ideas have been the foundation for later vocation improvement hypotheses that centre upon the relationship between people and occupations or workplaces. **(Sharf, 2006).**

Despite the fact that Parsons' thoughts on options for a career were first published in 1909, the concept of career decisions and the term "career decision-making" were not fully recognised until the 1950s. Many countries' employment regulations and social environments changed dramatically in the 1950s and the ensuing years. People sought improved job prospects as a result of these changes **(Inkson, 2007).**

2.2 Career-Decision-Making Theoretical Approaches

This segment initially looks at mental ways to deal with professional dynamics, focusing especially on two significant speculations: a hypothesis of professional characters and workplaces **(Holland, 1959)**. Later it considers sociological ways to deal with vocation dynamic, zeroing in explicitly on three hypothetical methodologies: self-viability **(Bandura, 1977),** social learning hypothesis of profession dynamic **(Krumboltz, 1979)** and social-psychological profession hypothesis **(Lent, Brown and Hackett, 1994)**. This part then, at that point closes with general uses of these hypotheses.

Hypothetical ways to deal with professional dynamics depend on two significant hypothetical points of view of vocation decision and advancement: mental and sociological **(Brown, 2002).** Mental methodologies try to portray or clarify the manner in which people settle on professional choices dependent on singular components which incorporate character, interests, capacities also, work fulfilment on the grounds that these variables essentially impact the manner in which people act, think, and react to settling on professional decisions. Then again, sociological methodologies try to foster a vocation dynamic interaction that permits people to consider the significance of an assortment of variables before their professional dynamic. Sociological put together speculations centre with respect to two main considerations; segment and natural **(Johnson and Mortimer, 2002)**. Segment factors allude to sex, identity, and the financial status of the family. Natural components allude to social impacts, like the effect of relatives, school companions, local area esteems and practices, the workplace, family associations, the work market structure and the monetary climate.

2.2.1 Career Decision-Making Psychological Approaches

Two early and compelling hypotheses of profession dynamic endeavored to apply mental ways to deal with assistance people settle on profession choices: the hypothesis of professional characters and workplaces by **(Holland, 1959)** and vocation secures by **(Schein, 1978)**.

(Holland, 1992) studies to help people to discover harmoniousness among themselves and the idea of a task, this hypothesis recommends that human conduct relies on both character and the climate in which the individual lives and the way they put themselves out there, their inclinations and their qualities through work decisions and encounters).

For instance, reasonable character types like to participate in the exercises or undertakings related with the orderly control of items, instrument, machines and creatures, and don't have to work with others. Fitting professional decisions for sensible character types could identify with mechanical, agrarian or specialized abilities. While imaginative character types like to take part in exercises or assignments related with less construction, like language, workmanship, music and show **(Holland, 1992)**.

For instance, an investigation of saw character and workplaces among college bookkeepers in Nigeria **(Afolabi, 1996)** tracked down that most of the administrators saw their character as insightful which, as per Holland's hypothesis, is an assignment arranged individual who is thoughtful and likes to thoroughly consider things as opposed to act indiscreetly. This character type appeared to lean toward occupations related to research, listing, order, etc. Curiously, library clients saw the bookkeepers' workplace as requiring a social direction since clients anticipated that librarians should discuss well with library clients. The examination presumed that this incongruence between custodians' apparent character and their workspace could prompt occupation disappointment. It was also assumed that people will be happier with their jobs if they choose workplaces that fit their personalities and interests, and that the more incongruence between their workplace and their personalities and interests, the lower the likelihood of vocation satisfaction. This examination features the effect of the connection among character and workplace on people's vocation fulfillment and in the more drawn out term, all things considered, profession fulfillment will influence people's future vocation dynamic.

Holland's six-character types are likewise a valuable rule for assisting people with understanding their character and professional interests and giving them the freedom to settle on a sane occupation choice that could prompt vocation fulfilment **(Hogan and Blake, 1999).**

In this manner, Holland has classified people into six character types: reasonable, insightful, creative, social, venturesome and ordinary and he clarifies how these character types are fit to specific workplaces **(Sharf, 2002).**

John Holland presented the hypothesis of professional characters and workplace in 1959 and accentuated the significance of the fit between professional decisions and workplaces **(Spokane, Luchetta and Richwine, 2002).**

For instance, the assessment of Holland's character types among youthful dark South African people **(Toit and Bruin, 2002)** utilizing multidimensional scaling examination tracked down a helpless fit between the information and Holland's model.

it assists businesses to give representatives proper workplaces which increment representatives' vocation fulfillment and obligation to an association **(Baruch, 2004).** Simultaneously, the idea of profession secures seems valuable for assisting people with discovering compatibility between their vocation directions and workplace **(Ituma and Simpson, 2006).**

As a result, the study found that the result may not have been appropriate in particular social circumstances, such as among South African teenagers. An analysis in China using Holland's six-character kinds corroborated this conclusion (Leong and Tracey 2006). This investigation inferred that Holland's six character types are more applicable in a Western setting.

It was created from Parsons' perspective on the professional decision, recommending people ought to get themselves and the idea of occupations and afterward discover compatibility between these two elements **(Kidd, 2006).**

2.2.2 Research on Theories of Career Choice

Although the conceptual framework approaches career choice developed from various theoretical foundations–personality Holland's types and work environment (1959), **(Schein's, 1978)** career anchors, **(Bandura's, 1977)** self-efficacy, **(Krumboltz's, 1979)** social learning theory of career decision-making, and **(Lent, Brown, and Hackett's, 1994)** social cognitive career theory–they are frequently combined or used in conjunction with other theories to understand how individuals make decisions. This study is noteworthy because it emphasises the effect of these theoretical methods as well as the numerous ways in which the theories may be utilised to broaden the knowledge of the interrelationships of factors that influence career choice.

Another research **(Järlström, 2000)** looked at the association among Finnish business students, there is a link between career expectations and the Myers-Briggs Type Indicator. using Schein's career anchors, a theory that examines people' talents or expectations related to their possible profession. The MBTI is a personality test that identifies different types of people's judgement and behaviour in the workplace **(Sharf, 2006).** According to the findings, there is a link between job aspirations and personality, as pupils who have the same career anchor have comparable personality types. Further research should be done to see if this association may be utilised to predict professional choice, according to the findings.

The personality types and work environment hypothesis of Holland, for example, emphasises the importance of personality and work environment congruence and the effect of personality on career preferences. As a result, this method may be used to forecast whether or not a person will pursue a given professional path. However, one study focused on the influence of familial history on the emergence of the entrepreneurial personality type done by Holland. **(Schröder and Schmitt-Rodermund, 2006)** to better understand how individuals develop certain job preferences. This study discovered that an individual's family past influenced the formation of an entrepreneurial personality and that family background may be utilised to predict enterprising interest patterns.

In a research that merged Holland's six personality types with the social cognitive career framework, the interplay between personality, career decision-making self-efficacy, and commitment of Chinese students' job choice process was explored **(Jin, Watkins and Yuen 2009)**.

2.2.3 Perspectives of Employee

According to this study, workers' self-efficacy perceptions may impact their choices to follow or leave a certain job. It also revealed that the better an employee's perceived self-efficacy was, the more confident they were in their capacity to attain their professional objectives. Personality has also been discovered to influence career choices. Managers in the hotel business are drawn to occupations that allow social contact, according to research on the link between personality and work desire among hospitality professionals **(Stone and Ineson 1997)**. They're also pragmatic, preferring short-term practical solutions over long-term strategic planning.

Research of management attitudes toward activities in the hospitality industry **(Waryszak and King, 2001)** came to a similar conclusion, revealing that deskwork is despised by most front-line hotel managers, who prefer hands-on activity. Despite the significance of these personal attributes, **(Watson, Buchannan, Campbell, and Briggs, 2003)** found four factors that employees thought affected their career choices inside a company. These factors include the organization's capacity to provide a job that is meaningful (for example, the possibility of learning a new set of skills, growing in their professions, and having their work recognised by others); fair and appropriate remuneration; adequate employment security; and the quality of personal connections (Management team support, strong relationships and friendliness with coworkers, and fair working hours). Previous research has shown the influence of various work environments and organisational rules on employees' career decision-making. Supervisors, coworkers, salary, possibilities for advancement, and morale, for example, were important variables in research of characteristics connected with the impact of the work environment on small company employees' job satisfaction in the United States **(Davis, 2004).** Having an impact on employee work satisfaction. Low job satisfaction among workers, according to the study, might have a psychological influence on their attitude toward working in the organisation and lead to a lack of passion and interest in work. This study suggests that if employees are unsatisfied with their work environment, they are less likely to be committed to their careers and may seek employment elsewhere.

The relevance of personality and job expectations was underlined in these two research. The mismatch between these is likely to lead to career unhappiness in the long run. Another individual element that is thought to be relevant in professional decision-making is a gender difference. According to a survey of charity retail managers **(Broadbridge and Parsons, 2005),** the most appreciated parts of their jobs for both male and female managers were a sense of pride for doing something important and job autonomy. Female executives also believed that their position allowed them to better balance work and family obligations. The impact of family obligations on female employees is demonstrated in this study, as well as how this might alter their job choice.

Another study that looked at the link between demographic variables and works satisfaction among healthcare professionals discovered the opposite impact **(Kavanaugh, Duffy and Lilly 2006).** The results of this poll show that senior employees are content with existing occupations. Employees' judgments that their working experiences were valued and that they were appropriately paid for their efforts appeared to be connected to this result. These two studies illustrate how employee self-efficacy and work satisfaction are influenced by organisational support. Low self-efficacy and professional satisfaction are likely to have a negative impact on their dedication to the company's career.

In one investigation of the influence of age discrimination policies and support on employees in large organisations **(Rabl, 2010)**, it was discovered that senior employees (50 years and older) perceived their age as being more likely to adversely impact their career within the organisation than younger employees (30-40 years).

Employees over 50 who believed they lacked organisational support also reported a fear of failing. As a result, management support may have an impact on the self-efficacy of older employees, resulting in a decline in their commitment to their jobs.

Furthermore, a study of the influence of location on ex-pats working in London **(Dickmann and Mills, 2010)** found that London is a place where employees' professional performance may be enhanced. This is due to London's reputation as a worldwide corporate hub. As a result, working in London may help people improve their learning, skill development, career progression, and lifestyles. This study emphasises the relevance of location and emphasises that workers may choose a certain location above others if it is seen to provide a better environment for career advancement and success to meet lifestyle demands. As can be seen, a multitude of factors can influence an employee's career advancement. Gender, age, perceived self-efficacy, family responsibilities, compensation, teammates and organizational commitment, and the workplace atmosphere are all things to think about. These characteristics can help or impede employees' professional happiness and success, as well as affect their career choices at various stages of their life.

(Kichuk et. al. 2019) researched that, employees who aren't considered for a hotel's talent pool are frustrated, distrustful of the company, and have poor career growth aspirations. The research was carried out in a hotel chain where strategies are one of the top objectives, but the findings may differ in other hotel chains.

(Sarwar and Muhammad, 2020) conducted a survey of hotel sector personnel to gather data. Incivility was also shown to be a major mediator, although mediation of discrimination was not. The findings are critical for hotel managers who want to increase organisational performance by adjusting their methods. For academics, this study provides food for thought by examining elements that detract from organisational effectiveness rather than focusing solely on those that improve it.

2.2.4 Employee' Perspective on Job satisfaction and Career Progression

Work satisfaction plummeted when preconceptions for the job were not satisfied. ''Reality shock" **(Hughes, 1958)** happened at times.

"The joyful emotional condition resulting from one's employment being judged as accomplishing or supporting the fulfilment of one's job values," according to the definition. **(Locke, 1969)**. Early empirical investigations by **(Porter and Steers, 1973)** and **(Muchinsky and Tuttle, 1979)** indicated that there is a negative correlation between work satisfaction and the likelihood of employee turnover.

When employees are happy at work, they are more likely to be steady, productive, and successful in achieving organisational goals **(Jessen, 2011)**. Job satisfaction is defined as an individual's total emotional orientation toward the employment position they are currently filling **(Kalleberg, 1977)**.

Pre-employment expectations, perceived work qualities, leadership concerns, and age were all found to predict job satisfaction **(Williams and Hazer, 1986)**. Job satisfaction was found to have a large and beneficial impact on organisational commitment, which lowered employees' intentions to quit and, as a result, reduced turnover.

Employees' work life and the successful utilisation of staff inside businesses are both dependent on job happiness **(Koeske, Kirk, and Rauktis, 1994)**.

(Lam, Zhang, and Baum, 2001) In the hotel' business, high staff turnover has become one of the primary issues. According to various studies, employee turnover is connected to job satisfaction and the importance of job factors reported by workers. The study looks at the relationship between demographic characteristics of hotel personnel and job satisfaction, as well as the importance of occupational determinants. According to the study's findings, employee demographic traits and the six Job Descriptive Index (JDI) categories differ substantially. As a strategy to improve job happiness, training and development programmes, particularly for newcomers and highly educated employees, as well as a comprehensive quality management approach, are advocated.

After such an interaction, employees' expectations were altered. depending on the job's reality. Job satisfaction increased when job-related expectations were satisfied during the shift. Employee job happiness was significantly influenced by perceived levels of job re-utilization and higher degrees of work participation, payment satisfaction, management support, and career changes, according to Rayton's (2006) empirical research.

Job satisfaction may be predicted using employee ratings of the work environment, organisational support, and employment status (Patah, Zain, Abdullah and Radzi, 2009).

Because an organization's culture may influence employee happiness, (Jackson and Hua, 2009) advocated that because job happiness has a substantial influence on personal life fulfilment, it is important to consider employees' needs while measuring employee satisfaction. (Heller, Watson, & Ilies, 2006; Pasupuleti, Allen, Lambert, & Cluse-Tolar, 2009).

Job satisfaction was described by Locke (1976), quoted in (**Rehman, Khan, and Lashari, 2010**) as a consequence of the range of particular satisfactions and dissatisfactions that he or she experiences as a result of the evaluation of numerous characteristics of work.

(Brown and Lam, 2008) differentiated between a global and a faceted approach to work satisfaction. Job satisfaction is defined by the global method as employees' sentiments about their jobs, whereas the facet approach considers growth, compensation, benefits, supervision, coworkers, the work itself, organisational environment, and working circumstances **(Biggs and Swailes, 2006); (Fichter and Cipolla, 2010)**.

Thus, job satisfaction is described as a subjective and emotional response to various elements of one's employment, as well as an emotional state resulting from an evaluation of one's position, as well as the characteristics and demands of one's work **(Jessen, 2011).**

Employees that are happy are more productive and stable, and they have a favourable attitude toward the company's goals **(Aziri, 2011)**.

(Pang and Lu, 2018) The study looked at how motivation affects work satisfaction and organisational effectiveness in the Taiwanese industry. Financial performance aspects such as return on assets, turnover growth rate, and profitability were positively influenced by employers' salaries and job performance. Non-financial performance variables like productivity and service quality were also affected.

(Okumus, Chaulagain, and Giritlioglu, 2019) This study looks at the impact of job stress and job satisfaction on hotel employees' emotional and exterior eating practices. It also considers how the body mass index (BMI) influences the proposed links. The data for the study came from 372 hotel workers in Antalya, Turkey, who worked in 10 four- and five-star hotels.

(Stamolampros et al. 2019) investigated that an improvement in work satisfaction of one unit is linked to a 1.2 per cent to 1.4 per cent rise in Return on Assets (ROA). A unit rise in the career advancement rating is associated with a 14.87 per cent reduction in the chance of an employee quitting the organisation.

2.2.5 Employee's Perspective on Employee's Benefits and Career Progression

(Mochama, 2013) looked into the impact of providing equal benefits to employees on their job satisfaction. The target population for KPC's Eldoret branch was 180 employees. For 49 workers, stratified random sampling was employed, and for 6 senior management personnel, purposive sampling was used. A questionnaire, document analysis, and interview schedules were used to collect data. According to the findings, there is a favourable relationship between equitable employee perks and employee work satisfaction. Additionally, there was a link between equitable employee benefits and greater productivity and profitability.

Financial rewards are again an important factor that is directly linked with employee job satisfaction. **(Bustamam, Teng, and Abdullah, 2014)** find out that The incentive system includes both money and non-financial advantages. Choosing the appropriate rewards for employees has always been a difficulty in human resource management. Many hotels are unable to establish which kind of incentives are most helpful in improving employee job satisfaction. The purpose of this study was to look at the link between incentives and work happiness, as well as the sorts of rewards that impact employee satisfaction. In this study, base pay hikes (financial) and recognition (non-financial) were explored. Employees who work as Front Desk Assistants at four- and five-star hotels are on the front lines. Malaysia was chosen as the study's sample. A total of 150 questionnaires were issued, with 132 being collected and analysed. In this research, four assumptions were assumed and evaluated. Correlation and multiple regression analysis were used to examine the data. The findings indicated that financial incentives (r=0.819**) and non-financial rewards (r=0.740**) are both positively and substantially related to work satisfaction.

(Jaworski et al. 2018) Part-time hotel employees were polled to see if the training approach and duration had an impact on job satisfaction. It was also evaluated the influence of advantages and incentives received, as well as training satisfaction, on employee commitment. Training satisfaction was found to be influenced by on-the-job training and work shadowing.

Hotel management strategies that contribute to corporate performance are known as human resources management (HRM). **(Ashton, 2018)** focuses on soft HRM techniques and draws on commitment and motivation theories. The findings give a broad framework for academic and management approaches to the labour and skill-shortage challenges.

High staff turnover has been a source of worry for hoteliers and academics alike. **(Yao et al. 2019)** intends to investigate the psychological advantages that influence employee attitudinal and behavioural loyalty in the hotel industry. The three elements of corporate commitment need employee trust and satisfaction as antecedents.

Another researcher **(Koo, Yu, Chua, Lee, and Han, 2020)** discussed that in the hotel industry, there are emotional benefits (compliment, opportunity, empowerment, and recognition), material rewards (promotion, certificate, incentive, and special leave), and job satisfaction, burnout, affective commitment, job performance, and turnover intention, as well as job satisfaction, burnout, affective commitment, job performance, and turnover intention. A quantitative strategy was employed in combination with a field survey method. According to a multiple regression analysis, emotional and financial incentives, as well as their dimensions, have a role in the development of affective commitment, work performance, and turnover intention.

2.2.6 Employee's Perspective on Technological Advancement and Career Progression

Not only rewards but new technologies and employees' competencies also have a significant relationship with their satisfaction level. Hotels are now working on many software and applications and it is mandatory for employees to update themselves for new technologies. Many times employees are not very happy with the technologies used by a specific hotel either technology is too old or the hotel did not focus to upgrade their technology for smooth functioning of operations and ease for employees.

As investigated by **(Lo and Darma, 2000)** many businesses continue to spend heavily on their information technology (IT) capabilities in order to increase operational efficiency and retain market competitiveness. This article analyses hotel workers' differing perspectives on the influence of organisational IT investment on (a) employee IT usage, (b) employee satisfaction with IT systems, (c) changes in employee performance, and (d) hotel organisational performance. A study of 945 hotel employees in Bali, Indonesia was conducted to determine their perceptions of IT's an organisational effect. The findings revealed that there were substantial disparities in employee perceptions based on age, educational level, hotel position, and individual income. These findings show that while top management may believe that investing in IT is desirable, employees may have differing views on what the true advantages of IT are. Managers should give special attention to influencing the attitudes of workers, who ultimately determine whether an organization's IT capabilities are put to use, in order to fully realise the potential of their IT investment.

2.2.7 Concept of Employee Workload and Job Satisfaction

It refers to the amount of labour a worker is allocated to or anticipated to do over a set period of time. The phrase "employee workload" refers to the perceived link between the quantity of mental processing skills or resources necessary to execute a task and the length of time it takes to complete it. **(Hart and Staveland, 1998)**.

Controlling workloads in an organisation becomes critical due to the tendency for workloads to fluctuate between workers in different departments of an organisation, as well as within the same department. The technique of changing staff workloads to bridge the gap between present and predicted workloads is known as workload management **(Van den Bossche et al., 2010)**.

Workload management, according to the company, "allows business-critical applications to get the attention they deserve while other applications run as resources become available; provides the resources needed to plan for changes in business workloads; and makes the system more adaptable and responsive to changing environments." **(Dasgupta, 2013)**.

Employee volume of work is a crucial component of efficiency and retention **(Rajan, 2018)**, and if that is lower than the actual workload, it will arouse lethargy as well as provide possibilities for them to be unproductive and start engaging in non-productive activities such as group politics, negatively impacting their performance. Employee workload is influenced by a variety of variables, including the severity of job requirements **(Nwinyokpugi, 2018)**.

In another study **(Inegbedion, Inegbedion, Peter, and Harry, 2020)** looked, workplace workload balance and job happiness are viewed by employees in different ways. Its purpose was to see how employee perceptions of task balance influenced job satisfaction. 764 personnel from eight multinational firms and two private Nigerian institutions were randomly recruited for the research. The findings show that comparing workloads with colleagues and aligning roles with competencies have a significant impact on employees' perceptions of workload balance and job satisfaction, that organisational staff strength has a significant impact on perceptions of workload balance, and that employees' perceptions of workload balance have a significant impact on job satisfaction.

2.2.8 Workload Perception and Employees' Areas of Specialisation

(Pearlman and Schaffer, 2013) studied on short- and long-term solutions for coping with labour difficulties. In the hotel and tourism industries, staff turnover is an issue, contributing to both direct and indirect costs. (e.g., recruiting, employment, and training) (e.g., increased working hours and worse customer satisfaction). This article highlights prospective Incumbent Worker Training Program advantages (e.g., lower training expenses, lower payroll taxes, greater employee retention, and engagement), which could motivate businesses in the hotel and tourism industries should commit to a long-term human resource management strategy. Employees are placed in roles and jobs that are designed for them by organisations. As a result, employment positions are unique to each company **(Ford and Jin, 2015).** Individual employees fill the positions formed by organisations based on their functions, which are determined by their vocation and specialisation. As a result, roles are unique to people since their vocations serve as a universal organisational foundation for the development of positions and work roles in organisations. Employees with the same job title in multiple businesses generally have comparable job characteristics. As a result, some of the inequities that most individual employees face are influenced by differences in working circumstances between occupations. As a result, it is theoretically reasonable that work characteristics at the occupational level of analysis have been demonstrated to predict work-related outcomes **(Ford, 2012); (Ford and Jin, 2015),** despite the fact that job responsibilities vary greatly within these professions.

(Dhevabanchachai, 2017) investigates the hotel training center's in-house internship with two clearly defined goals: (1) to explore students' preconceptions prior to taking the internship and compare them to their perception afterwards; and (2) to investigate student interns' capabilities and knowledge, as well as the impact of in-house internship on students. The results of the focus group interview and story narrative of the brief open-ended questions are analysed using a qualitative method known as content analysis. The outcomes of the study emphasise the need of requiring require in-house internships in the Tourism and Hospitality Management curriculum. The study also found that in-house internships may help students prepare for real internship experiences in the hotel industry, as well as their educational value in the tourism and hospitality curriculum.

(Q.et al. 2021) studied the most influential elements influencing hotel trainees' work satisfaction and future ambitions in China A survey of hotel management students from three Chinese institutions was used to collect data. Internship achievements, mentorship and assessment, interpersonal relationships, compensation, hotel features, hotel internship programming, and curriculum requirements are the seven factors that influence students' satisfaction with their internship experience and career intentions, according to factor analysis. Intern satisfaction was influenced by internship achievements, curriculum requirements, hotel internship programming, mentorship, and assessment, according to regression results, while career intention was influenced by curriculum requirements, interpersonal relationships, and internship achievements. The research provides factual data to help in the creation and implementation of hotel internship programmes.

(Giousmpasoglou, 2021) explained about the hotel internship experience might be seen as a turning moment in a student's decision to continue in the business or quit. The purpose of this article is to demonstrate the happiness of hospitality students with internships and how that affects their career intentions. A study of 172 students was performed to look at internship satisfaction in 4 and 5-star hotels as a significant factor of career intention. The data show that the genuine working circumstances and the learning experience were the most important elements influencing students' satisfaction. Long work hours, low pay, and a lack of coordination were all mentioned as major obstacles, but all participants agreed that internships were a beneficial opportunity to connect their education with real-world experience. Student satisfaction in hospitality internship programmes, according to this study, can have a direct beneficial impact on graduates' career intentions. It also recommends that educational institutions keep the practical/applied components of hotel management programmes in order to produce skilled, knowledgeable graduates.

2.3 Women Employee' Perception for Career Progression

2.3.1 Women Employee' Perception about Career in the Hotel Industry

Women's status in society is reflected in the roles they play in institutions such as the family, politics, and other social organisations. A similar sentiment is echoed in the corporate world. **(Chaudhary and Gupta, 2010)** mentioned that women currently hold greater positions of authority in Indian industry than in the past. The Indian hospitality business follows a similar path. However, in comparison to their demographic proportion, women hold fewer posts than men. Despite a variety of legislative and policy initiatives made by the government, this continues to be the case. The vertically typical "Gender Pyramid" is also present in this lower level occupation, with little chances for advancement for women and top leadership positions occupied by males.

The hotel industry is equally attracted to males and females and everyone wants to make their career in the industry. It came to notice much time that industry does not treat their male and female employees equally and female employees does not get sufficient opportunities for career progression. As a result **(Santero-Sanchez, Segovia-Pérez, Castro-Nuñez, Figueroa-Domecq, and Talón-Ballestero, 2015)** a gender-specific examination of employment quality is required. The researchers develop and build a composite index of work quality, which combines objective job security criteria into a single variable to discover probable gender variations in employment quality. Unlike other job quality comparisons that focus just on income, the composite indicator created emphasises workweek duration in an area where part-timing has a particularly negative impact on women. Women have lower-quality occupations than males, according to the findings, and the gender disparity worsens with age.

Another research by **(Russen, Dawson, and Madera, 2021)** looks at hotel managers' opinions on hotel employee promotions based on the promoted employee's gender, organisational fairness, and perceived gender discrimination against women. With a sample of 87 hotel managers, the study used an experimental design (female versus male promoted). Mediation and moderated mediation analyses were used to examine the data. The findings showed that procedural and distributive justice modulates the influence of the promoted employee's gender on women's perceptions of gender discrimination.

2.4 Student Perspective

There has been an increasing interest in understanding how university students and graduates make career selections in recent years. These findings are likely to lead to the development of strategies that will allow young people to make rational career and job decisions **(Hodkinson, 1998)**.

This information might be useful to educational institutions in terms of facilitating students' job possibilities and assisting them in achieving career success after graduation **(Jeffreys, 2004).**

Another element that tends to influence students' career decisions is the ability to gain job experience. Work experience, it has been suggested, gives students the opportunity to try out different occupations and learn about their future careers. As a result, individuals have more confidence in making career decisions **(Smith, Dalton and Dolheguy, 2004).**

Students with minimal work experience, on the other hand, are less likely to be able to make career choices or selections based on their passions rather than their abilities. **(Feldman and Whitcomb, 2005)**. As a result, students with work experience were more likely to make better career choices than those without.

Students enrol in specific courses for a number of reasons, according to several research looking at the first issue. Students picked the course based on their interest in the topic, employment chances, and career prospects after graduation, according to a study on variables thought to be relevant by young college students **(Maringe, 2006).**

The influence of one's family history on a student's job choice is equally significant. (**Mau, Ellsworth, and Hawley, 2008**) discovered that 16 per cent of graduating teachers who reported strong tenacity and contentment with their teaching career had teachers like mothers, and 7% had teachers as fathers. As a consequence, this study discovered that the graduates' professional likeness to their parents, particularly their mother, was a factor in predicting job happiness and career perseverance.

The socioeconomic origins of students may also influence their career preferences and choices. According to research on professional decision-making behaviour among students from working-class households, a lack of funding aid might have a negative impact on students' decision-making or educational choices **(Greenbank and Hepworth, 2008)**. They may also have limited job possibilities because they may not be able to find work outside of their hometown.

These findings corroborate research on why travel and hotel students chose to study in Australia **(O'Mahony, Whitelaw and McWilliam, 2008)**. Many students were discovered to make judgments primarily on the institution they would attend rather than which degree they would be admitted into. Some students, on the other hand, chose to enroll in a particular course because of strong job prospects and the industry's reputation, and their past work experience in the field. These studies tend to show that students choose careers based on employment prospects, labour demand, their personal economic background, family or family support, and a desire to seek further education, rather than their own professional preferences. Some researchers have looked at why students pick a specific career after graduation. According to these researches, there are a number of factors that influence students' job choices. For example, in a study of the link between gender and students' inclinations to pursue an entrepreneurial profession **(Schwarz et al. 2009)** boys students are more interested in launching their own business than girls, according to the study. Gender inequalities among accounting students were also evident. **(Danziger and Eden 2007)**, with Male students are more enthusiastic about starting a business than female pupils. Female students said that they prefer working as employees since they recognise that the nature of their occupations may make balancing work and family duties difficult if they marry. This gender-work association is also in line with the past findings on employee career decision-making.

According to **(Yang, Partlow, Anand, and Shukla, 2014)** viewpoints about industry experts and educators, this study evaluated the relevance of general and technical managerial abilities required of hotel management graduates in India. Both participant groups in India received a self-administered questionnaire. The findings of this study revealed six generic management abilities and seven technical managerial competencies.

Although the growth of the hotel sector might result in additional job possibilities, it is sometimes criticised for providing low-skilled and low-paying positions. The focus of this article is on final-year students who have finished their industrial training and are ready to work in hotels. According to the findings, students are neither positive nor adverse to hotel occupations. The data also suggest that there is a desire to work in the hospitality sector or to learn more about it. **(Pol and Patil, 2015)**. This sector desperately needs to attract and hire competent and trained workers. However, owing to parental influence, a large per centage of Hospitality and Tourism Management (HTM) undergraduates fail to make career selections to work in the tourism business.

In addition,**(Zhang, Rashid, and Mohammed, 2016)** has created a value conceptual model that investigates the theoretical linkages between motivational variables and students' career choices in the hospitality industry. This study contributes to the body of knowledge by explaining the relationship between two motivating characteristics and students' career choices, as well as determining the moderating role of an internship programme in that relationship.

(Kahuthu Gitau, Gesage, and Mugambi, 2017) examined that the impact of demographic variables, individual background factors, and career result expectations on undergraduate hospitality students' career decisions. The majority of participants (69%) were females, and many (71.9%) had entered the hotel industry with only a high school education. Surprisingly, the majority of respondents (85.4 per cent) planned to pursue a job in the hotel business after graduation. Among the relevant variables (gender, individual background characteristics, and career outcome expectations), multiple regression findings indicated that career outcome expectations were the most significant predictor. According to the researcher, hospitality practitioners should give more possibilities for students to directly experience a genuine sector position, such as field trips, internships, and part-time work.

As a result, it is critical to give a value conceptual1model that elaborates on the theoretical links that exist between two parental variables and the career goals of the hotel and tourism management students. **(Zhang, Rashid, and Mohammed, 2017).**

2.4.1 Students' Internship Experiences and Impact on Career Decision Making

(Kaşli and İlban, 2013) The goal of this study is to identify the challenges that undergraduate students face during internships and to analyse their future intentions to work in the tourist sector. The study also considers if the difficulties encountered during the internship programme have an impact on the students' desire to work in the tourist industry in the future. Convenient sampling was used to choose third- and fourth-year undergraduate students from two separate institutions who had finished their internships for the study, and the surveys were performed with 330 of the 550 eligible individuals. Internship difficulties have four dimensions, however, they may also be regarded in two sub-dimensions from a commercial standpoint. According to the findings of this study, interns are only given extremely limited employment rights, interns are considered as cheap labour, and the service industry does not contribute to interns' professional advancement.

According to **(Robinson, Ruhanen, and Breakey, 2016)** students in the hospitality and tourism industries regularly change their minds about their future paths. This qualitative research looks at how having a certain form of work experience, such as an internship, affects students' career choices and ambitions. While the majority of respondents modified their career goals as a result of their internship, these changes were more of a business movement than a rejection. Many participants claimed that their goals had changed from pursuing a job in hospitality to pursuing a career in industry, however, this was not the case.

(Tarmazi et al. 2017) Many graduates of hospitality courses are currently hesitant to enter the sector once they have completed their studies. This occurrence is said to be due to the graduates' hardships throughout their internship programme, which altered their view of the sector. Because the students are dissatisfied with the programme, this will have a negative impact on the sector. The goal of this study is to see if there is a link between motivation and work experience in terms of student happiness after completing an internship programme. This research had a total of 93 participants. The link between the variables was determined using Pearson Correlation Analysis. All of the criteria were shown to be significantly connected to the student's satisfaction with the internship programme.

Students in the hospitality and tourism industries regularly change their minds about their future paths. This qualitative research looks at how having a certain form of work experience, such as an internship, affects students' career choices and ambitions. While the majority of respondents changed their career objectives following the internship, these shifts were more of a movement within the business than a rejection. Many participants claimed that their goals had changed from pursuing a job in hospitality to pursuing a career in industry, however, this was not the case. **(Qu, H., Leung, X. Y., Huang, S. S., and He, J. 2021)** studied to determine the most influential elements influencing hotel trainees' work satisfaction and future ambitions in China A survey of hotel management students from three Chinese institutions was used to collect data. Internship achievements, mentorship and assessment, personal relations, compensation, hotel features, hotel internship programming, and curriculum requirements are the seven factors that influence students' satisfaction with their internship experience and career intentions, according to factor analysis. Intern satisfaction was influenced by internship achievements, curriculum requirements, hotel internship programming, mentorship, and assessment, according to regression results, while career intention was influenced by curriculum requirements, interpersonal relationships, and internship achievements.

2.4.2 Students' Perspective on Social Status and Their Impact on Career Decision Making

There is a well-established relationship between parental socioeconomic background, adolescent career desires, school performance, and adult social status accomplishment, according to researchers **(Ashby and Schoon, 2010)**. Tested a path model linking family background factors (such as family social status and parental aspirations) and individual agency factors in adolescence (in particular, career aspirations and ambition value) to social status attainment and earnings in adulthood using data from an 18-year British follow-up study. According to the research, the value of one's ambition is proportional to one's adult salary. That is, as adults, young people who prioritise professional growth earn more money than their less motivated peers. The data also demonstrate a relationship between teenage professional goals and adult social status achievement, suggesting that family background variables, adolescent career desires, and ambition value all interact to impact adult social position attainment and remuneration.

(Metheny and McWhirter, 2013) had studied to learn more about how social status and family support influence young people' job choices in college. On 270 undergraduate students, we evaluated a route model for predicting career decision self-efficacy and job-related outcome expectancies. Financial position, social standing, family support, and purposeful family career-related contacts were all factors that were taken into account. The outcomes of social cognitive career development are connected to both family status and family support, according to the findings.

(Penny Wan, Wong, and Kong, 2014) has worked on students' perspectives toward career opportunities and employment intention are influenced by their perceptions of the nature and social standing of hospitality jobs, as well as their income expectations. According to a poll of hospitality students in a major Asia Pacific tourism destination, the perceived nature of the profession had no meaningful link with career possibilities. Furthermore, students' social standing influenced their opinions of job possibilities, and students' commitment to the sector was influenced by their beliefs of future prospects. The author goes on to examine the data' theoretical and practical consequences, as well as the moderating influence of pay expectation. The findings of this investigation give a more complete picture.

The hotel and tourism industry requires a high number of employees to work in the industry instead of that **(Anandhwanlert and Wattanasan, 2016)** investigated that the hotel business is sometimes chastised for producing low-skilled, low-paying employment with minimal work satisfaction. This study was based on a previously validated model to better understand the underlying elements that influence students' willingness to work in the tourist and hospitality sector. Six elements, such as type of job, social standing, career possibilities, promotion opportunities, physical working conditions, income, and fringe benefits, are likely to impact commitment, according to the literature study around the issue.

As previously said, students choose job options based on a variety of variables, including parental responsibilities and socioeconomic status, which can have a good or negative influence on their career choices.

2.5 The Impact of Culture on Career Perceptions

The impact of culture on professional decision-making has revealed that culture underpins people' basic judgements, which shape their behavioural intents, expectations, and results related to specific occupations in their cultural environment **(Hofstede, 2001)**.

(Li and Leung 2001) discovered that females were regularly promoted to positions of management. These executives, on the other hand, said that their workplace culture compelled them to take on additional family responsibilities as a mother, wife, and career for their parents. Female managers found it difficult to combine their work and family duties as a result of these cultural influences, resulting in low job satisfaction and slow career development to senior management positions in the organisation. These studies show that gender has an influence on job advancement and that in some societies, males have an easier time progressing in their careers. Even when men and women have equal job possibilities inside a company, societal beliefs about gender roles can have an impact on career advancement. As a result, women and men may create separate career choices at various stages of life.

A career is a series of plans, intentions, ambitions, and actions, and the culture that surrounds this process may either assist or hinder people in making professional decisions and attaining success. **(Young, Valach and Collin, 2002)**. As a result, career and culture are inextricably linked.

According to studies on career decision-making, the elements thought to be in various cultures, people make diverse decisions about their careers. are comparable. The influence of age has been discovered in research in the Netherlands **(Kooij et al., 2008)**.

Gender has been found to have an influence in Austria **(Mayrhofer et al. 2008); (Mooney and Ryan, 2009)**.

In research conducted in Taiwan **(Horng and Lee, 2009)**, and the United States **(Zhang and Wu, 2009)**, family variables (i.e. parents, family duties, and socioeconomic background) were discovered

Studies in India **(Gokuladas, 2010)** and the United Kingdom have discovered the influence of location **(Dickmann and Mills, 2010)**. However, other research has shown that the amount to which these characteristics influence people's job decisions is influenced by their cultural settings.

As previously said, culture may have a considerable influence on an individual's professional decision-making. People make use of their cultural interpretation to make reasonable job selections, despite the fact that comparable elements are considered to affect professional decision-making.

In conclusion, this section has examined and analysed a variety of study results on professional decision-making. As can be observed, professional decision-making is a complicated process, and prior research suggests that employees and students evaluate a variety of criteria while making career selections, including age, perceived self-efficacy, family obligations, employment, and the business climate. These characteristics either help or hinder employees and students achieve professional happiness and success, and they have an impact on their following career choices.

2.6 The Impact of Job satisfaction on Career Perception

As investigated by **(Lo and Darma, 2000)** many businesses continue to spend heavily on their information technology (IT) capabilities in order to increase operational efficiency and retain market competitiveness. This article analyses hotel workers' differing perspectives on the influence of organisational IT investment on (a) employee IT usage, (b) employee satisfaction with IT systems, (c) changes in employee performance, and (d) hotel organisational performance. A study of 945 hotel employees in Bali, Indonesia was conducted to determine their perceptions of IT's an organisational effect. The findings revealed that there were substantial disparities in employee perceptions based on age, educational level, hotel position, and individual income. These findings show that while top management may believe that investing in IT is desirable, employees may have differing views on what the true advantages of IT are. Managers should give special attention to influencing the attitudes of workers, who ultimately determine whether an organization's IT capabilities are put to use, in order to fully realise the potential of their IT investment.

(Lam, Zhang, and Baum, 2001) In the hotel' business, high staff turnover has become one of the primary issues. Employee turnover is linked to work satisfaction and the relevance of job aspects perceived by employees, according to several research. The study investigates the link between hotel workers' demographic features and job satisfaction, as well as the relevance of occupational factors. Employee demographic characteristics and the six Job Descriptive Index (JDI) categories differ significantly, according to the findings of the study. Training and development programmes, particularly for newcomers and highly-educated staff, as well as a whole quality management approach, are proposed as ways to increase job satisfaction.

Job satisfaction is defined by the global method as employees' sentiments about their jobs, whereas the facet approach considers growth, compensation, benefits, supervision, coworkers, the work itself, organisational environment, and working circumstances **(Biggs and Swailes, 2006); (Fichter and Cipolla, 2010).**

Employment satisfaction, thus, is defined as a subjective and emotional response to many aspects of one's job, as well as an emotional state arising from an assessment of one's position, as well as the features and demands of one's work **(Jessen, 2011).**

When employees are content, they are more productive and stable, and they have a positive outlook on the organization's goals **(Aziri, 2011).**

(Mochama, 2013) looked into the impact of providing equal benefits to employees on their job satisfaction. The target population for KPC's Eldoret branch was 180 employees. For 49 workers, stratified random sampling was employed, and for 6 senior management personnel, purposive sampling was used. A questionnaire, document analysis, and interview schedules were used to collect data. According to the findings, there is a favourable relationship between equitable employee perks and employee work satisfaction. Additionally, there was a link between equitable employee benefits and greater productivity and profitability.

Not only rewards but new technologies and employees' competencies also have a significant relationship with their satisfaction level. Hotels are now working on many software and applications and it is mandatory for employees to update themselves for new technologies. Many times employees are not very happy with the technologies used by a specific hotel either technology is too old or the hotel did not focus to upgrade their technology for smooth functioning of operations and ease for employees.

Financial rewards are again an important factor that is directly linked with employee job satisfaction. **(Bustamam, Teng, and Abdullah, 2014)** find out that The incentive system includes both money and non-financial advantages. Choosing the appropriate rewards for employees has always been a difficulty in human resource management.

Many hotels are unable to establish which kind of incentives are most helpful in improving employee job satisfaction. The purpose of this study was to look at the link between incentives and work happiness, as well as the sorts of rewards that impact employee satisfaction. In this study, base pay hikes (financial) and recognition (non-financial) were explored. Employees who work as Front Desk Assistants at four- and five-star hotels are on the front lines. Malaysia was chosen as the study's sample. A total of 150 questionnaires were issued, with 132 being collected and analysed. In this research, four assumptions were assumed and evaluated. Correlation and multiple regression analysis were used to examine the data. The findings indicated that financial incentives (r=0.819**) and non-financial rewards (r=0.740**) are both positively and substantially related to work satisfaction.

(Okumus, Chaulagain, ands Giritlioglu, 2019) The effects of job stress and job satisfaction on hotel employees' emotional and external eating patterns are investigated in this study. It also looks at how the body mass index (BMI) affects the hypothesised connections. The study's data came from 372 hotel employees in Antalya, Turkey, who worked in ten four- and five-star hotels. To evaluate the study hypotheses, structural equation modelling (SEM) was used. According to the findings, job stress has a substantial beneficial impact on both emotional and external eating habits of hotel employees, whereas job satisfaction has a significant favourable impact on only external eating behaviours.

Another researcher **(Koo, Yu, Chua, Lee, and Han, 2020)** discussed about the emotional benefits (compliment, opportunity, empowerment, and recognition), material rewards (promotion, certificate, incentive, and special leave), job satisfaction, burnout, affective commitment, job performance, and turnover intention that exist in the hotel business. A quantitative technique was utilised in conjunction with a field survey strategy. Multiple regression studies indicated that emotional and financial incentives, as well as their dimensions, have a role in the development of affective commitment, work performance, and turnover intention.

2.7 Employees of the Hotel Industry

2.7.1 The Significance of Human Resource Management in Hotels

The difference between a successful and well-run hotel and one that is not is down to the efficacy of its human resources management, which is critical to its success. According to **(Pereira-Moliner et al. 2012)**, Human resource management is crucial for satisfying guests and preserving the hotel's service quality by guaranteeing the proper amount of hotel workers, the right sort of staff, and the right time for providing services. Human Resource Management is the most essential department for hotel staff, and human resources serve as the only interface between clients and hospitality businesses. **(Chin and Tsai, 2013; Kim and Lee, 2013)** backed up this conclusion, claiming that hotel workers may have a major influence on service quality and the environment. As a consequence, selecting dedicated and enthusiastic personnel for diverse hotel tasks is crucial.

According to (**Karatepe, 2013)**, it is the responsibility of HR management to ensure that efficient and welcoming individuals are employed as hotel employees who are capable of dealing with a broad range of people or visitors from various parts of the world. In contrast, (**Chinand Tsai, 2013)** believes that not only engaging efficient staff is crucial for sustaining a nice culture in hotels, but also retaining such employees for a longer duration is equally critical for HR management. This not only saves hotels money by eliminating the need for regular employee recruitment and training in hospitality. However, it is difficult for hotels or management to keep staff because the majority of them work part-time to make quick money and have no intention of staying in the industry in the future. In this regard, (**Hanzaee and Mirvaisi, 2013)** noted that because the majority of hotel employees do not choose to work in hotels as a long-term career objective, they opt to stay and work as hotel employees for a shorter length of time in order to make some money.

High staff turnover in the hotel sector is caused by a bad work culture or work ethics, as well as linguistic difficulties **(Chin and Tsai, 2013)**. There are, however, a number of methods that HR management may minimise the chance and intent of people leaving their hotel employment. As a result, HR management in the hotel sector is quite important in this regard. It can retain hotel personnel for extended periods of time by providing effective training and incentives. The hotel's HR management may encourage employees to stay longer at their jobs by offering a clear progression plan to enhance the level of hotel services **(Molina-Azorn, et al, 2015)**. Employee engagement and promotion are also critical issues in the hotel sector, emphasising the necessity of HR management in the hotel industry. Employee retention is higher in hotels that take different steps to enhance the status of workers and give hospitality training so that they may learn the essential skills for welcoming and communicating with a broad spectrum of guests.

2.7.2 Improving Service Quality via Employee Management and Skill Development

Organizations must concentrate on personnel management and skill development in order to improve service quality and customer service. There are numerous ways to improve employees' knowledge and abilities so that they can provide better products and services to consumers. The following are some examples of how to manage people and enhance their skills:

- **Encourage innovation:**

Employees' innovative ideas must be encouraged, and they must have the flexibility to work independently. This will assist in the development of personal talents as well as methods for improving customer service. Employees can accept new changes and use innovations to improve their personal working efficiency and the overall performance of the company as a result of innovation and technological progress **(Kim and Lee, 2013).**

- **Training and development**

Employees can use the training programme to develop their own knowledge and abilities in order to increase their efficiency. According to **(Chen, 2013)**, organisational training is helpful in providing accurate information about the pricing and quality of items, as well as techniques to service consumers and engage with them to gain a better understanding of their tastes and preferences. The organization's training programme also allows employees to work as part of a team and communicate with others in order to expand their expertise. As a result, training is critical for providing high-quality products to clients.

- **Collaborate to solve problems:**

Employees in the hotel sector may use collaborative working practices to address organisational challenges and delight consumers by offering efficient products and high-quality service in line with market trends. This working practise and experience, according to (**Hanzaee and Mirvaisi, 2013**), helps staff build problem-solving abilities and is helpful for the hotel sector in resolving client concerns as their demands change. Employees benefit from personal experience and contact in order to handle client concerns and please them through quick service.

- **Open communication and information sharing:**

Open communication among hotels, restaurants, and catering companies facilitates the exchange of information and expertise regarding consumer needs, product and service prices and quality, and market trends. Employees can also detect organisational difficulties with open communication (**Molina-Azorn, et al. 2015**). Sharing knowledge via communication is an excellent approach to improve one's own abilities in order to provide better service and please consumers.

- **Continual feedback is essential:**

Managers must get constant feedback in order to keep track of their workers' performance. Annual performance evaluations aid in the planning of training and development, promotion, reducing performance difficulties, and developing personal abilities in order to achieve corporate objectives. The feedback on performance and the performance strategy. Employees are further motivated by relevant compensation and incentives to enhance their own efficiency so that they can please consumers.

As a result, in order to offer superior quality products, hotel personnel must be managed and their abilities must be developed. The skills and knowledge of employees have an impact on their performance in terms of improving service quality and satisfying consumers.

2.7.3 Employee Empowerment's Impact on the Hotel Industry

Employee empowerment encourages workers to work independently and participate in the organization's decision-making process. Employee empowerment allows them to execute high-risk actions without jeopardising the organization's aim, quality, purpose, or vision. Self-reward, open communication, collaborative working practise, teamwork, problem-solving abilities, and encouraging workers' creativity are the greatest ways to empower them, according to **(Chin and Tsai, 2013)**. Another method to empower employees is to solicit input from them in order to enhance organisational service rather than simply monetary compensation. The management strives to promote the employees' freedom, provides flexible working hours, and recognises their efforts to motivate and empower them, as employee empowerment helps to enhance the organisational service. Employee empowerment contributes to higher production and lower costs by encouraging creativity and innovation. As employees' ownership of their job grows, so does their efficiency, and they are better equipped to provide quality goods services to consumers. Employees that are empowered strive to take more risks in order to increase their chances of success. Employee empowerment also enables workers to use creative ideas in order to satisfy consumers. Employees, according to **(Kim and Lee, 2013)**, are the ones who can recognise the genuine needs of the consumers, and greater employee creativity helps to enhance the utility of the customers. The approach and other methods of empowering staff have a significant influence on increasing service quality and satisfying consumers through efficient service delivery. As a result of employee empowerment, productivity, work satisfaction, quality assurance, technological innovation, and motivation all improve.

2.8 Employees Performance

2.8.1 Employee performance effectiveness in terms of service quality

Employee performance is essential in delivering excellent products and services to customers based on their requirements and preferences, thus the organization's service quality is determined by their performance. Reliability, responsiveness, empathy, tangible products, and assurance, according to **(Pereira-Moliner et al. 2012)**, enable employees to work successfully so that they may please consumers. As a result, staff performance is critical in providing great service to customers.

Employees can better grasp consumer perceptions of the company's products and services thanks to effective working procedures. It is the obligation of staff to cater to the needs and preferences of customers, and it is important to perform effectively in order to improve overall efficiency in the hotel industry. Working with others or in a team, on the other hand, is important to increase staff productivity and has a significant influence on the hotel industry's service quality. Collaboration also aids staff in resolving cross-cultural difficulties inside the business and providing great service to consumers according to their demands.

Cooperation between consumers and workers, on the other hand, allows employees to provide the appropriate products and services to the right customers after determining their genuine preferences and requirements.

According to (**Chiang and Hsieh, 2012**), open communication between consumers and workers allows customers to voice their opinions while also allowing employees to provide better service by knowing their genuine needs.

Employees are driven to work better in order to receive extra compensation as a result of performance-related pay, assessment, respect, open communication, and collaboration among team members. According to (**Karatepe, 2013**), the service quality is determined by the employee's performance and communication style in determining the customer's perception. Thus, it is critical to have efficient staff that can manage clients and assist them in resolving their difficulties in order to give great service.

2.8.2 Hospitality Management Employee Motivation and Performance

High levels of customer satisfaction and regular visitor loyalty are enhanced by a nice hotel atmosphere or service environment, efficient operations, and a strong knowledge of client expectations.

The relevance of non-financial incentives in motivating employees is clearly explained by psychology researches that offered numerous theories and studies of employee motivation **(Chiang and Hsieh, 2012).**

Employees who have been taught and worked hard to offer the services that hotels guarantee to clients, according to **(Kim and Lee, 2013)**. Furthermore, workers' communication with visitors is critical for addressing their urgent requirements, and therefore guest-employee interaction is a key component in customer satisfaction. In hotels, the performance of employees is crucial for providing high-quality services and increasing customer satisfaction **(Karatepe, 2013).** The hotel's workers, at all positions, represent the hotel, thus a guest who feels ignored or mistreated will have little motivation to stay more or return. Customers decide the value and quality of hotel services, according to **(Hanzaee and Mirvaisi, 2013)**, thus Employees in charge of providing the visitor experience should be not only taught but also driven to meet the guests' service quality and value expectations. HR managers, as well as hoteliers, play a critical role in educating and encouraging hotel employees to provide excellent customer service experiences. Appropriate compensations, cash awards, recognition programmes, and other methods used by hotel HR management to motivate workers or staff are effective ways to motivate employees or staff in the hotel business **(Karatepe, 2013).**

Money is the most common incentive of employee performance, according to **(Hanzaee and Mirvaisi, 2013)**, i.e. the direct money that employees receive from management for their customer service. Indirect compensation is also provided by the hotel management in the form of health insurance and deferred compensation, which puts money in the hands of employees in the form of benefits or services in order to incentivize them to perform better **(Chin and Tsai, 2013).**

Non-monetary benefits and incentives, recognitions, respect at work, a pleasant working environment, and other factors can help hotel staff become more engaged and motivated to offer better or higher-quality services **(Kim and Lee, 2013).** Recognition programmes such as "Star of the Month," gift certificates, gift vouchers, and appreciation in the form of awards are all examples of non-monetary incentives used to inspire employees. Non-monetary incentives are largely used by hotel management resources to improve employee performance and service quality, which increases customer satisfaction.

2.9 Conclusion

The total literature study demonstrates the importance of staff performance in enhancing service quality and customer happiness. The literature study focuses on a variety of factors such as job satisfaction, workload, social standing, and perks, among others, that impact employee, intern, and student perceptions of their career growth in the hotel business, both directly and indirectly. The literature also aids in recognising the importance of human resource management, which has a significant influence on service quality and customer happiness.

The literature also gives an opportunity to learn about the developing hotel business and its advantages, employee empowerment, and the development of one's own skills and knowledge, as well as get practical experience with the impact of workers' performance on the hotel industry's service quality. To explain the workers' motivating aspects. As a result, the literature aids in the formulation of research hypotheses and the effective completion of the study.

CHAPTER -III
3 RESEARCH METHODOLOGY

3.1 Introduction

This chapter explains the research plan as well as the processes for gathering and examining method data. It goes through the data collection techniques, sample design, operational definitions of constructs, measurement scales, and data analysis methods utilized in this study.

3.2 Research Design

The quantitative research approach has been used in the investigation.. Quantitative research is a type of business study that combines empirical evaluations with numerical measurement and analytical techniques to achieve research goals **(Zikmund et al., 2010)**. This technique has chosen because we have conducted our research by collecting samples from the hotel sector in India's four regions: north, west, east, and south. From the northern area of India, we have chosen certain cities, such as Shimla, Srinagar, Dehradun, Chandigarh, and Delhi/NCR. From the western area, there are Jaipur, Ahmedabad, Pune, and Mumbai. Bengaluru, Hyderabad, Chennai, Kochi, and Goa are located in India's southern area, whereas Bhuvneshwar, Patna, Ranchi, Kolkata, and Darjeeling are located in the eastern region. The questionnaires have been sent out to see if there's a link between employee perception and career advancement. It will also examine the different factors which are important for creating positive or negative perceptions among employees for making a career in the hotel industry. Each survey responder used numeric scales to score a variety of criteria in their business. SPSS software is used to examine the numeric information gathered from the surveys. The quantitative research technique has been chosen since in study includes a high number of participants. Their viewpoint has been quantified into a scale and transformed their opinion into a result using SPSS software due to a large number of respondents.

Aside from that, this study was based on causality. Researchers can utilise explanatory research to derive causal findings and look for cause-and-effect relationships (Zikmund et al., 2010). In other words, there has to be a reason (cause) for anything to happen (an effect). The goal of this research is to determine what is driving India's skilled personnel deficit in the hotel industry.

3.3 Data Collection Methods

In order to conduct a survey for this research, both primary and secondary data were required.

3.3.1 Primary Data

Primary data is first-hand information gathered by researchers on the aspects that are relevant to the study's goal (Sekaran, et al., 2010). Because it takes time to contact respondents and perform the survey, primary data gathering takes longer than secondary data collection. The perspective of our targeted responder was the most important piece of information we used in our inquiry. We solicited their input by mailing them a self-administered survey. A questionnaire has been produced which is containing questions about the study's independent and dependent variables, and we've requested comments from our intended respondents. First-hand data, or primary data, refer to the information received from respondents.

3.3.2 Secondary Data

Secondary data is information obtained from sources other than the researchers performing the present study **(Sekaran et al., 2010)**. The internet has been used to access journals authored by other scholars for this research. The government websites are being used to get statistics and gathered information from pertinent websites. When compared to the main data, secondary data is easier to get. Aside from that, we also used critical information from publications recommended by other writers that were pertinent to our research. For instance, we used journals from Science Direct, Emerald and Elsevier, as well as open-access peer-reviewed journals. In addition, we did our studies using the E-library database provided by our university.

3.4 Sample Design

To answer the research topic, we need a sample to complete our survey properly and accurately. Sampling is the method of selecting representative people, objects, or events from a target population **(Sekaran et al., 2010)**.

3.4.1 Target Population

The target population, according to **Sekaran et al. (2010)**, is the group of people that researchers are interested in studying. Because the research focuses on the impact of employee perception on career decisions and advancement, the hotel industry has been chosen as the focus. As a result, our target demographic is employees in the hospitality industry and current students of hotel management as they are also employed in the hotel during internships periods. It is important to know their perception as well for industry because they are future manpower. We'd like to gather information from hotel employees who work in operational departments and students of hotel management who either did or completed their internship in the hotel industry, to learn about their careers decisions perceptions.

3.4.2 Sampling Frame and Sampling Location

The sampling frame represents all of the elements in the population from which the sample is drawn (Sekaran et al., 2010). In order to conduct our study, we'll need a list of target demographics to contact.

Due to a lack of information, it was difficult to collect a comprehensive list of people employed in the hotel industry. This is partly due to the fact that the organization considers employee information private and confidential, and partly due to the fact that the total number of hotel employees is just too large for us to get their information and the same is applicable with students who are studying in different hotel management institutes. For this study, employees and students of 5-star hotels in India were given questionnaires.

In 2018, the number of foreign tourists arriving in India grew to 10.56 million, up from 10.04 million in 2017. FTAs grew at a pace of 5.2 per cent in 2018 over 2017, compared to 14.0 per cent in 2017 over 2016. In 2018, India received 1.2 per cent of all international visitor arrivals. In 2018, India ranked seventh in the Asia Pacific Region, with 5.0 per cent of international tourist arrivals. The number of domestic tourist visits to India in 2018 was 1854 million (revised), up from 1657 million in 2017, representing an 11.9 per cent increase. Every year, a large number of visitors visit these sample places.

3.4.3 Sampling Elements

Employees who work at hotels in these areas were the respondents to this research. Employees in the hotel's operational divisions are specifically targeted as survey respondents. Employees functioning as departmental leaders, executives, or supervisors, and at the assistant level are examples of operational departments such as the Front Office, Housekeeping, F & B Service, Food Production and Sales and Marketing. This is because we wanted to hear from employees about how hotel rules, leadership, and motivation affect employee perception from the top down. Employees' perceptions of career progression are important in achieving corporate objectives. Similarly with hotel management students, who had the experience to work in industry during their industrial training or vocational training. The survey wants to hear from students about their perceptions related to the hotel industry and how they see the industry as a career option.

3.4.4 Sampling Techniques

Convenience sampling technique has been utilized to pick respondents from our target group for this study. A non-probability sampling includes convenience sampling. Non-probability sampling denotes that no element in the target population is assigned any odds of being chosen as a research sample (Sekaran et al., 2010). Convenience sampling, on the other hand, refers to gathering information from a target group depending on whether or not the target responder is convenient or accessible to complete a questionnaire with us (Sekaran et al., 2010). Our sampling locations for this study were cities from all four regions of India. Employees are typically preoccupied with their own jobs because the hotel business is

As a result, we chose to adopt this sample approach to avoid interfering with their jobs as a result of our research.

3.4.5 Sampling Size

According to FHRAI, the number of employees working in 5-star hotels in India is approximately 2,50,000 plus including interns, and the number of workers working in the operational department of a five-star hotel is around 1,80,000 (Estimated data). On other hand, total students in hotel management are approx. 35,000 as per the National Council of hotel management, Ministry of tourism. According to (Sekaran et al. 2010), a total of 384 people are needed to complete the survey. These respondents were drawn from India's four regions. A total of 656 sets of questionnaires were distributed to employees and students working in our sampling locations as part of our research. However, only 452 sets (332 sets belong to a hotel employee and 120 sets belong to students who are doing an internship in the industry) of questionnaires have been received, and the remainder were either unsuitable because they were not completed/responded to or did not meet the standards.

3.5 Research Instrument

3.5.1 Pilot Study

Before complete research has been conducted, a pilot study was conducted. Pilot research was carried out on a smaller scale in order to develop a more detailed confirmatory investigation **(Arain et al. 2010)**. Before conducting the complete study, a pilot study was conducted as a preliminary study to confirm that the questionnaire is reliable and that the study is practical.

A self-administered technique has been used to disseminate our surveys throughout the pilot research. The following is the implementation timeline for our pilot study:

Table 3-1: For Pilot Study

Date Taken	Activity
9th August 2021 - 31st August 2021	30 sets of questionnaires have distributed and received.
24th August 2021	Arrange the data from the gathered questionnaires.
29th August 2021	SPSS software was used to enter the data.

Source: Self-developed for research

A pilot study has been completed with 45 hotel workers in our selected sample locations from August 9 to August 31, 2021. As previously stated, we disseminate our questionnaire via self-administered questionnaires. Before delivering the questionnaire to respondents, they were infromed about the objective of this study, as well informed them the reason this survey is being conducted.

Aside from that, we've ensured that our respondents have enough time to complete our surveys. This is to guarantee that people do not answer the questions in a rush, which might lead to their selecting the incorrect option. We returned our surveys to them once they had completed them. The average time it took for responders to complete the questionnaire was 15 to 20 minutes.

The data has been structured, that we obtained from the respondents on August 24' 2021, and over the next 5 days, until August 29, 2021, the data collected will be keyed into the Statistical Package for the Social Sciences (SPSS) software to assess the questionnaire's reliability.

3.5.2 Full Study

Employees working in hotels in selected locations in four areas of India were targeted in our survey in order to complete the whole study. During the whole research, a total of 656 sets of questionnaires were delivered. To deliver surveys to our respondents, we utilized the self-administered questionnaire technique.

The following is the strategy we followed to perform the entire study:

Table 3-2: Schedule for Full Study

Date Taken	Activity
1st September 2021	Obtain information on the individuals who will be responding to our survey. Obtain information on the individuals who will be responding to our survey.
3rd September – 10th September 2021	Distribution of questionnaires
18th September 2021	Collection of questionnaires
30th September 2021	Analyze the data and provide a proposal for the research findings.

Source: Self-developed for research

Information has acquired on our targeted respondents till September 1, 2021, to make the distribution procedure easier. The questionnaires have been prepared and distributed in Google form and shared with target respondents through various platforms such as personally visiting a few hotels, email, Facebook, Linked In, and others from September 3rd to

September 10th, 2021, and collected back until September 18th, 2021, after respondents filled them out. We have given our responders enough time to read and complete the questionnaire with complete comprehension. The data obtained from respondents have been entered into SPSS software version 22 till September 30, 2021, and the findings of this study have been proposed.

3.6 Constructs Measurement (Scale and Operational Definitions)

Constructs measurement is used to demonstrate the questionnaire's validity. The following are the three sections of the questionnaire:

Section A: Demographic Profile

Section B: Perception of Hotel Industry Professional (Employees and Hotel Management Students)

    B1: Job Satisfaction

    B2: Employee Benefits

    B3: Training and Development

    B4: Employee Perceptions

Section C: Career Progression or Career Making Decision

All of the above factors are utilized to investigate the link between hotel industry professionals' perceptions and their career decisions. The total number of questions in the questionnaire is 39. Section A, in particular, consists of eight questions that capture respondents' basic demographic information. Seven questions, six questions, six questions, and six questions make up sections B1, B2, B3, and B4. These factors are based on workers' and students' perceptions of their company, which professionals use to make career-related decisions. Finally, there are six questions meant to assess individuals' professional decision-making abilities.

Aside from that, all of the items in the questionnaire are designed in a fixed-alternative style, which gives respondents a restricted number of alternatives. Respondents are requested to express their thoughts by picking one of the alternatives. The major reason for only including fixed-alternative items in the questionnaire is to make it easier for respondents to complete it. Aside from that, researchers may use this format to compare responses from various respondents.

Section A: Demographic Profile

The first section of our questionnaire is dedicated to gathering demographic data from our target responder. We need demographic data to understand the nature of our respondents and to determine whether there is a likely link between demographic data and our research subject. In the first portion, seven questions have been created. The following are the subjects covered in each question:

Table 3-3: Questions of Demographic Profile

No of Question	Topic Covered
1	Gender
2	Age
3	Education
4	Experience
5	Type of Employment
6	Region of Workplace
7	Department

Source: Develop from research

The gender of the responder is the first question on the questionnaire. This question is designed in a nominal scale style, with two options for respondents to choose from male or female. This is a typical research topic that many academics utilize in their studies. The purpose of including this question in the survey is to see whether there are any gender variations in terms of perception and career decisions.

The age of the responders is then included in the questionnaire. Because the age groups can be ordered from smaller to larger, the question is structured on an ordinal scale. The following are some of the possibilities we offered in this question:

1. Below 25 years old
2. 26-35 years old
3. 36-45 years old
4. 46-55 years old
5. More than 55 years old

We divided the alternatives into five categories in order to obtain more precise and particular information about the respondents' ages.

The third question concerns our respondents' educational attainment. As the degree of education can be organized from the lowest qualification, Senior Secondary, to the greatest qualification, Post Graduate, an ordinal scale is utilized. The inquiry is intended to assess the amount to which our respondents possess certain information, skills, and talents, among other things. The following are the options we provided in the survey:

1. Senior Secondary
2. Diploma
3. Graduate
4. Post Graduate

The fourth question is related to employee working experience. Working experience in the industry is an important tool to analyze. The working experience can be ordered from less to more, the question is structured on an ordinal scale. The following are the options we provided in the survey:

1. Less than 1 Year
2. 1-2 Year
3. 3-5 Year
4. More than 5 Years

The fifth question is related to the type of employment. As hotel industry recruit employees on different payroll bases and employee type of employment is also one of the major factors. This is again an important factor that must be covered in the study. The following are the options we provided in the survey:

1. Contractual
2. Permanent

The sixth question is to find out where our respondents work or what region they work in. As noted in the preceding chapter, our target respondents are individuals who work in India's northern, western, eastern, and southern areas. As a result, we provide our respondents the opportunity to choose from all four possibilities. This question is designed utilising a nominal scale. Each of these four zones has a value assigned to it in order to demonstrate differences between them, but the value contains no further information such as order or distance. We inquire about the respondent's workplace location or area because we want to see whether there are any disparities in employee perceptions and career decisions based on workplace location.Northern Region

1. Western Region
2. Eastern Region
3. Southern Region

In this step, we ask one final question about the department in which our target responders work. In this question, a nominal scale is utilised since the value assigned to each choice simply conveys differences between alternatives and cannot be ordered or used to determine the distance between them. Our target responders in the hotel sector might be from a variety of departments. Each department may be given distinct duties and execute various tasks. In the hotel sector, there are just five key operating departments. The following are the five departments listed in the questionnaire:

1. Front Office
2. Housekeeping
3. F&B Service
4. Food Production
5. Sales and Marketing

All of the above information provided by respondents working in the hotel business can assist us in understanding the demographic characteristics of hotel employees. As a result, it can help us gain a better understanding of how employees'/students' perspectives influence their career choices.

Section B: Perception of Hotel Industry Professional

After gathering demographic data from our target responder, the questionnaire's attention shifted to independent variables. Job satisfaction, employee benefits, training and development, and employee/student' perceptions are all independent variables described in the preceding chapter. A series of questions with a 5-point Likert scale is designed to measure how these independent variables influence employee/student career decisions. The 5-point Likert scale is employed because it improves the questionnaire's validity and standardization. It's critical to standardize the options in the questionnaire so that researchers can compare them across questions. Furthermore, the uniform option aids in providing a trustworthy response to the researcher. Here's an illustration of what each question's options are:

Strongly Disagree (SD)	Disagree (D)	Neither Disagree nor Agree (N)	Agree (A)	Strongly Agree (SA)
1	2	3	4	5

Each question will be graded on a scale of one to five, with one indicating significant disagreement, two indicating disagreement, three indicating neither dispute nor agreement, four indicating agreement, and five indicating strong agreement. The respondent can pick a number between 1 and 5 to indicate how much they agree or disagree with the statement in the questionnaire. A responder may select answer option "3" if they do not agree or disagree with a statement in the questionnaire. This demonstrates that the individual has no strong sentiments regarding the subject. Before each sub-part is presented, an overview of section B will be provided.

Table 3-4: Section B of Questionnaire

Sub Section	Question	Area Covered
B1	JS1	Provide insight about the enjoyable work.
	JS2	It is regarding about working pressure on employees.
	JS3	Regarding about the compensation.
	JS4	Regarding about the daily and family needs.
	JS5	Regarding about non-monetary rewards.
	JS6	Talks about leadership at workplace.
	JS7	Regarding about praise on workplace.

Sub Section	Question	Area Covered
B2	EB1	Accommodation facilities provided by organisation.
	EB2	About child care facilities.
	EB3	About pick up and drop facility.
	EB4	Regarding health incentives.
	EB5	Yearly increments.
	EB6	About meal during shifts.
	EB7	Regarding about praise on workplace.

Sub Section	Question	Area Covered
B3	TD1	Provide training opportunities
	TD2	Focus on employee's skills and knowledge
	TD3	Variation in training programs
	TD4	Frequency of training program
	TD5	Selection the area of training
	TD6	Employee development

Sub Section	Question	Area Covered
B4	EP1	Motivation of employees.
	EP2	Regrading employee efforts towards organisation goals.
	EP3	Employee's emotional connect with organisation.
	EP4	Regarding seeking better job opportunities.
	EP5	Regarding working environment.
	EP6	Behaviour of top managers.

Source: Develop from research

A question on job satisfaction is being developed in the first sub-section. This variable indicates how satisfied workers are with their working circumstances in the organisation. To assess the selected job satisfaction variable, six items have been developed. These items are being adopted from the government of Western Australia, the public sector commission.

The employee benefits variable is measured in the next section. This independent variable assesses the extent to which firms give monetary or non-monetary advantages to their employees in order to motivate them. This section contains six products that are being designed. These questions are being adopted from the government of Western Australia, the public sector commission.

The training and development variable is measured in the next section. This independent variable assesses how much training opportunities, training programmes, and long-term development are emphasized in employee training plans. This section contains six products that are being designed. Tseng et al. and Tabassi et al. provided the inspiration for these questions.

Six questions are being used to measure employee perceptions as an independent variable. This dimension assesses how satisfied members of the organization are with the overall policies followed by the company. The questions in this section are based on Natalie Wickham of Quantum Workplace.

Section C: Career Decision Making / Career Progression

The questions have been designed in this section to see how respondents felt about the criteria used to evaluate job options. Similar to the preceding section, a 5-point Likert scale is used to determine if respondents agree or disagree with the statements provided. Six questions were developed to assess the organization's effectiveness. In each question, the 5-point Likert scale example is as follows:

Strongly Disagree (SD)	Disagree (D)	Neither Disagree nor Agree (N)	Agree (A)	Strongly Agree (SA)
1	2	3	4	5

On a scale of one to five, respondents can score how much they disagree or agree with the statements. If a respondent strongly disagrees with a statement in the questionnaire, they might select "1." Respondents can choose "5" if they strongly agree with the statement. If respondents have no strong views about the statements in the organisational performance variable, they may choose "3" to indicate that they are neutral.

Below is the overview question in section C

Sub Section	Question	Area Covered
B5	CC1	Career satisfaction.
	CC2	Comparison current career with other industry careers.
	CC3	Regarding self-pride and career.
	CC4	Social esteem as hotel professional.
	CC5	Industry as a career option.
	CC6	Gender discrimination.

Source: Develop from research

Under the heading of career decision or progression, there are three dimensions: career satisfaction, social reputation as a career choice, and career comparison with other industries. There are a total of six questions in all three dimensions. These questions were adapted from the Western Australian Government's Public Sector Commission.

On the other hand, simultaneously, we have distributed and collected questionnaires to hotel management students who either had worked as interns or doing their internship in 5-star hotels. This questionnaire is also divided into 2 parts. We keep the questionnaire easy and short so that students do not find any difficulty to fill and provide responses. We asked a total of 24 questions in which 4 questions were related to their demographic profile and the rest 20 questions were related to their career perspective and desired working conditions. All questions in section B were based on a 5-point Likert scale.

Section A: Demographic Profile of Students.

Section B: Students perspective towards a career in the hotel industry.

3.7 Data Processing

Following the return of all surveys, several preparatory procedures must be taken to guarantee data quality and consistency. These data will be transformed into information and utilised for further analysis in order to evaluate hypotheses generated in the previous chapter. Data processing is crucial in our study endeavour since the accuracy and timeliness of the data might impact the research results (Malhotra, 2007). Data processes, according to Malhotra (2007), include various steps such as questionnaire verification, data editing, data coding, data transcription, data cleaning, and the process culminates in the selection of an appropriate data analysis method.

First and foremost, when respondents complete the survey form, we personally examine the questionnaires gathered. We have double-checked that all of the questionnaires we gather are complete, and we have discarded any that wasn't. We have come across several incomplete questionnaires at this point.

The data have been edited to verify that the surveys are accurate. Some respondents did not complete the surveys according to the instructions. These surveys are deemed invalid, and they must be removed. Aside from that, we discovered that two sets of questionnaires returned from respondents failed to answer six questions in Section B. As a result, these surveys were modified based on the overall pattern of their replies.

The modified data is given a number once it has been edited. According to Malhotra (2007), numerical numbers have been provided to each piece of data to make the data entry process easier. After that, the coded data have been entered into a computer. We entered the data into the SPSS version 22. During the data cleaning step, more comprehensive consistency checks have been performed using SPSS software. We looked for data discrepancies so that we might create more correct data for further analysis.

The choice of a data analysis strategy is the final stage in the data processing. We choose a data analysis method that can match the features of the data obtained based on previous work in developing our study project.

3.8 Data Analysis

3.8.1 Descriptive analysis

Descriptive analysis has been performed to summarise the results of our respondent's demographic profile. Descriptive analysis is used to transform raw data submitted by respondents into a format that makes it simpler for readers to comprehend, evaluate, and make decisions based on the data. A plan is put up to efficiently transform raw data into information in order to make use of the data obtained from our targeted responder.

In Section A of the questionnaire, there are eight questions pertaining to the demographic information of respondents. In terms of gender, we want to utilise a pie chart to represent the per centage of male and female respondents. Each gender is clearly displayed in a pie chart, allowing the reader to immediately grasp the proportion of each gender in the sample.

Aside from that, we have utilised frequency analysis and a bar chart to display the proportion of our targeted responders in each age category. The education group of our targeted responder, on the other hand, have been displayed using a pie chart. Frequency analysis and bar charts have been utilised to depict data obtained in terms of experience level, job location and type of employment of our targeted responder. Finally, we have created a bar chart to depict data collected on the departments in which our targeted respondents work.

3.8.2 Scale Measurement – Reliability Test

The internal consistency of respondents' responses is measured by the questionnaire's reliability. The word "reliability" refers to the extent to which a questionnaire is devoid of random error and capable of producing consistent results. Cronbach's coefficient alpha is the most often used measure for determining reliability in research. The direction and intensity of the linear relationship between the dependent and independent variables are shown by the coefficient alpha (α).

The greater the value of the coefficient alpha, the more reliable the questionnaire. The coefficient alpha value ranges from 0 to 1, with 0 indicating no internal consistency within the responses obtained from respondents and 1 indicating perfect consistency. According to Zikmund, coefficient alpha may be classified into the following categories:

Table 3-5: Rules of Thumb about Reliability Test

Coefficient alpha (α) value	Reliability
0.80 – 0.95	Very good reliability
0.70 – 0.80	Good reliability
0.60 – 0.70	Fair reliability
Below 0.60	Poor reliability

Adapted From: Zikmund, W. G., Babin, B. J., Carr, J. C., & Griffin, M. (2010). Business research methods (8th ed.). New York: South-Western/Cengage Learning.

According to the table, a questionnaire's reliability is regarded to be extremely excellent if the coefficient alpha value is between 0.80 and 0.95. Coefficient alpha values of 0.70 to 0.80, on the other hand, are considered to be reliable. The degree of dependability is rated fair dependable for the range with a coefficient alpha of 0.60 to 0.70. The degree of dependability is deemed bad when the coefficient alpha goes below 0.60.

After collecting data and opinions from 45 respondents, we conducted a pilot test. The opinions of these respondents are being input into SPSS software in order to assess the questionnaire's reliability. The following are the results of the pilot research after entering them into SPSS software:

Table 3-6: Reliability of Questionnaire (Pilot Study)

Construct	Coefficient Alpha Value(α)
Job Satisfaction	0.969
Employee Benefits	0.954
Training and Development	0.952
Employee Perception	0.953
Career Choice	0.965
Overall Reliability	**0.985**

Source: Develop from research

According to the result generated by SPSS software, the coefficient alpha value of job satisfaction, employee benefits, training and development, employee perception and career choice is 0.969, 0.954, 0.952 and 0.953 respectively. In another word, all independent variables have very good reliability in investigating the problems that we are intended to measure. On the other hand, the coefficient alpha value of a dependent variable, career choice is 0.965 which is considered to have good reliability. Apart from testing each individual variable in the questionnaire, we also test the reliability of the overall questionnaire. The coefficient alpha value of overall reliability is 0.985 which is considered to be very good reliable. Since the reliability of this questionnaire is quite high, so this questionnaire is considered to be suitable to be used in the full study.

3.8.3 Inferential Analysis

To evaluate the link between our independent and dependent variables, we utilised a Likert scale. Under the scale of measurement, a Likert scale is a sort of ratio scale. Because the ratio scale falls under this category, our variables are known to be metric in terms of measurement. To examine the link between metric variables, we use the Pearson correlation coefficient and multiple regression analysis as statistical approaches.

3.8.3.1 Pearson Correlation Coefficient

The Pearson correlation coefficient is a method for determining the degree of relationship between two variables. Its value can range from -1.0 to 1.0. (the University of the West of England, 2007). The correlation coefficient is denoted by the letter r. There is a perfect positive linear (straight-line) relationship when the value of r is 1.0. There is a perfect negative linear relationship or perfect inverse relationship when the value of r equals -1.0. As the value of correlation approaches one, the strength of association becomes stronger, while as the value of correlation approaches zero, it becomes weaker. The rules of thumb about correlation coefficient are shown below:

Table 3-7: Rules of thumb about the correlation coefficient

Coefficient Range	Strength of Association
±0.91 - ±1.00	Very strong
±0.71 - ±0.90	High
±0.41 - ±0.70	Moderate
±0.21 - ±0.40	Small but definite relationship
±0.00 - ±0.20	Slight, almost negligible

Source: Adapted from Hair, Money, Samouel and Page (2007). Research methods for business. John Wiley & Sons Ltd, pg. 358.

3.8.3.2 Multiple Regression Analysis

Numerous regression analysis is an analysis that uses an interval scale to examine the effect of multiple independent variables on a single dependent variable. (W. G. Zikmund, 2010) The following is the equation for multiple regression analysis:

$$Y_i = b_0 + b_1X_1 + b_2X_2 + b_3X_3 + + b_nX_n + e_i$$

The R^2 coefficient of multiple regression depicts the variance of the dependent variable when all independent variables are combined. (W. G. Zikmund, 2010) This equation can be used to examine the effect of each independent variable on the dependent variable. Each independent variable contributes a distinct per centage of variation in the dependent variable. Independent factors' effects on the dependent variable can be prioritized.

Multiple regression is used in our study to find employees' perceptions that have a significant impact on career decision making or career progression in the hotel industry. Researchers will be able to create a least-square regression equation and calculate the beta to rank independent variables from there.

3.9　Conclusion

This chapter concludes with a detailed description of the research design. The research technique for this study will be based on primary and secondary data sources that specify the research design within the sample frame. Each variable's measurement is addressed in detail, as well as data collecting and analysis methodologies. In chapter four, the planned data analysis will be explained in further detail.

CHAPTER – IV
4 DATA ANALYSIS

4.1 Introduction

In the previous chapter, we mentioned about our respondents for this survey were employees of hotels' core operational departments and students who are studying hotel management and have experience of internship during their curriculum. To cater for both respondents we distributed 2 questionnaires with different items. The chapter then moves on to describe the various constructs and their central tendencies. It is followed by an inferential analysis to illustrate how the dependent variable and the independent variables are related.

4.2 Descriptive Analysis

4.2.1 Demographic Profile of Respondents

Table 4--1: Respondent Demographics Profile (Employees)

Score		Per cent*
Gender	Male	52.40
	Female	47.60
Age	Below 25 Years	15.70
	26-35 Years	42.20
	36-45 Years	26.80
	46-55 Years	15.40
	55 Years and Above	0.00
Education	Senior Secondary	6.90
	Diploma	31.60
	Graduate	37.70
	Post Graduate	23.80
Experience	Less than 1 Year	5.10
	1-2 Year	43.10
	3-5 Year	25.30
	5 Year and More	26.50
Type of Employment	Contractual	16.90
	Permanent	83.10
Region of workplace	North region	22.30
	West region	35.50

	East region	18.10
	South region	24.10
	Front Office	21.40
	Housekeeping	21.40
Working Department	F&B Service	31.00
	Food Production	21.40
	Sales and Marketing	4.50
Willingness to work	Yes	60.20
	No	39.80

*Per centage excluded missing observations

4.2.1.1 Gender

Table 4--2: Frequency of Score of Gender, (N=332)

Score	f	Per cent
Male	174	52.4
Female	158	47.6

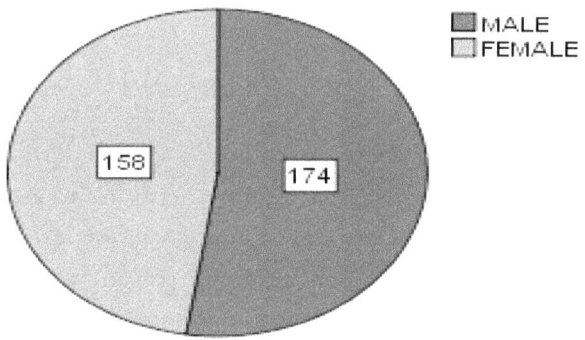

Figure 1 *Chart Representation of Gender*

The proportion of 332 female and male respondents who took part in the questionnaire survey is shown in Table 4.2 and Figure 1. Males made up (174, 52.3%) and females made up (158, 46.6%) of the questionnaires we obtained during the study.

4.2.1.2 Age

Table 4--3: Frequency of Score of Age, (N=332)

Score	f	Per cent
Below 25 Years	52	15.7
26-35 Years	140	42.2
36-45 Years	89	26.8
46-55 Years	51	15.4
More than 55 Years	00	00.0

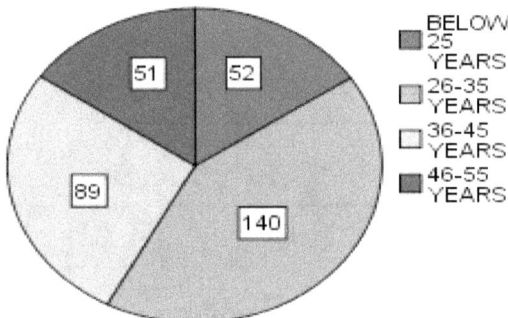

Figure 2 Pie Chart Representation of Age

The age distribution of our respondents is seen in Table 4.3 and Figure 2 above. A total of 332 people took part in this poll. It was discovered that (52, 15.7 per cent) respondents are under the age of 25, (140, 42.2 per cent) respondents are between the ages of 26 - 35, (89, 26.8%) respondents are between the ages of 36 - 45, (51, 15.4%) respondents are between the ages of 46 - 55, and no respondents are over the age of 55. According to the data gathered, the majority of those who took part in this questionnaire survey are between the ages of 26 - 35.

4.2.1.3 Education

Table 4--4: Frequency of Score of Education, (N=332)

Score	f	Per cent
Senior Secondary	23	6.9
Diploma	105	31.6
Graduate	125	37.7
Post Graduate	79	23.8

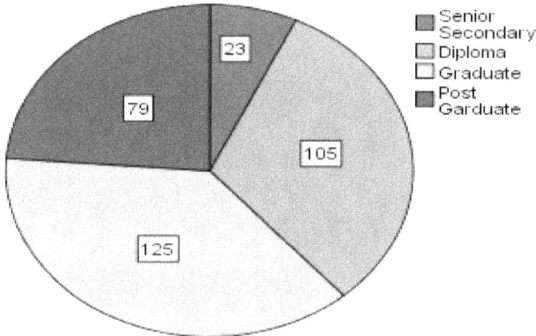

Figure 3 Pie Chart Representation of Education

The education level of 332 respondents in our survey was given in Table 4.4 and Figure 3. Among all respondents, 23 respondents have completed senior secondary school, 105 have a diploma in hospitality management, 125 have a bachelor's degree, and 79 have a master's degree. As a result, the per centages for these four categories are 6.9%, 31.6%, 37.7%, and 23.8 %, respectively. The majority of respondents in this study were either graduates or holders of a hospitality diploma, according to the data.

4.2.1.4 Experience

Table 4--5: Frequency of Score of Experience, (N=332)

Score	*f*	Per cent
Less Than 1 Year	17	5.1
1-2 Years	143	43.1
3-5 Years	84	25.3
More Than 5 Years	88	26.5

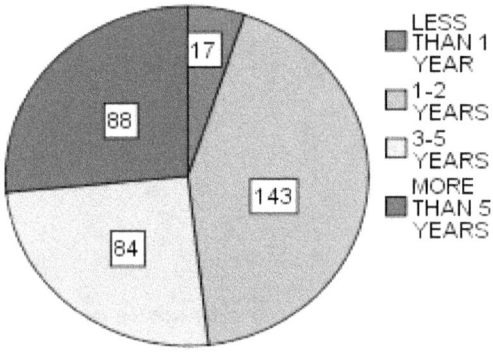

Figure 4 Pie Chart Representation of Experience

Employee experience in the hotel industry is illustrated in Table 4.5 and Figure 4. There were 17 respondents who had been engaged for less than a year, 143 who had been employed for one to two years, 84 who had been worked for two to three years, and the remaining 88 who had been employed for more than five years. Each of the categories has a proportion of 5.1 per cent, 43.1 per cent, 25.3 per cent, and 26.5 per cent, respectively. According to the data above, the majority of respondents to our questionnaire survey had worked in the hotel sector for one to two years.

4.2.1.5 Type of Employment

Table 4--6: Frequency of Score of Employment, (N=332)

Score	f	Per cent
Contractual	56	16.9
Permanent	276	83.1

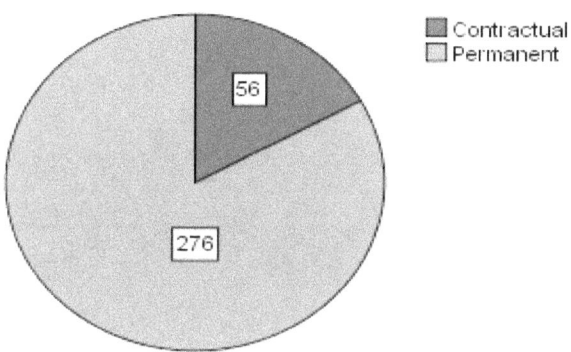

Figure 5 *Pie Chart Representation of Employment*

Table 4.6 and Figure 5 show inform about the employment type. There are total of 332 respondents of which 56 respondents were working in a hotel on a contractual basis and 276 employees were permanent and on the payroll of the hotel. The per centage for each category is 16.9% and 83.1% respectively.

4.2.1.6 Region of workplace

Table 4--7: Frequency of Score of Workplace, (N=332)

Score	f	Per cent
North Region	74	22.3
West Region	118	35.5
East Region	60	18.1
South Region	80	24.1

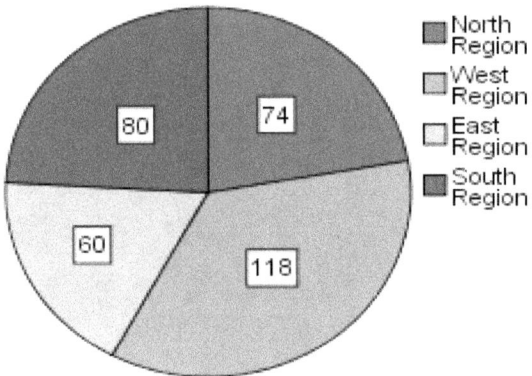

Figure 6 Pie Chart Representation of Region of Workplace

Table 4.7 and Figure 6 show information about the different regions of employees' workplaces. Out of 332 respondents 74 respondents were working in hotels situated in the northern region of India, 118 respondents were working with hotels which are situated in the western region of the country, 60 respondents were working in the eastern region and 80 respondents were working in southern region hotels. The table also inform about the per centage of respondents from region wise like 22.3%, 35.5%, 18.1% and 24.1%

4.2.1.7 Working Department

Table 4--8: Frequency of Score of Working Departments, (N=332)

Score	f	Per cent
Front Office	71	21.4
Housekeeping	72	21.7
F&B Service	103	31
Food Production	71	21.4
Sales & Marketing	15	4.5

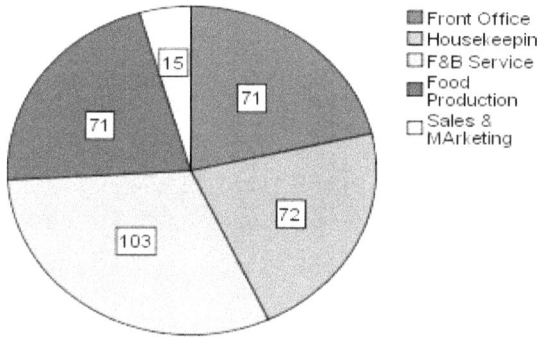

Figure 7 Pie Chart Representation of Working Department

Table 4.8 and Figure 7 had shown the departments in which respondents were working during the survey. Total 332 employees were surveyed, where 71 respondents were working in the front office department, 72 respondents took part from the housekeeping department, 103 respondents were part of the F&B service department, 71 were employed in the food production department and 15 were working in sales and marketing department. As mentioned in an earlier chapter we have chosen respondents who were working in the core operational departments in the hotel industry. Table 4.8 further shows the per centage of respondents which are 21.4%, 21.7%, 31%, 21.4% and 4.5% respectively. The table also indicates that mostly respondents are from the F&B service department and an almost equal number of respondents participated from the front office, housekeeping and food production department. The least number of respondents are from sales and marketing as many limitations are associated with the sales and marketing department.

4.2.1.8 Willingness to work

Table 4--9: Frequency of Score of Willingness to Work, (N=332)

Score	*f*	Per cent
Yes	199	59.9
No	133	40.1

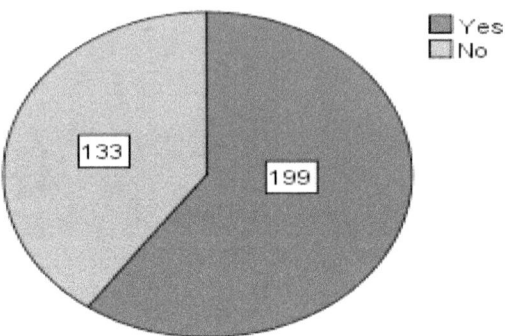

Figure 8 Pie Chart Representation of Willingness to Work

Table 4.9 and Figure 8 shows the frequency of willingness of employees to work in hotels. As table 4.9 indicates that the majority of respondents who are working in the hotel industry are willing to work in the hotel industry with (199, 59.9%) and (133, 40.1%) respondents are not willing to work in the hotel industry.

4.3 Descriptive Analysis (Interns-Students)

Table 4--10: Respondent Demographics Profile (Students)

Score		Per cent*
Gender	Male	54.16
	Female	45.83
Work Experience	Yes	90.00
	No	10.00
Year of Study	1st year	0.00
	2nd year	19.16
	3rd year	30.00
	4th year	50.83
Willingness to work	Yes	80.00
	No	20.00

*Per centage excluded missing observations

4.3.1 Gender

Table 4--11: Frequency of Score of Gender, (N=120)

Score	f	Per cent
Male	65	54.2
Female	55	45.8

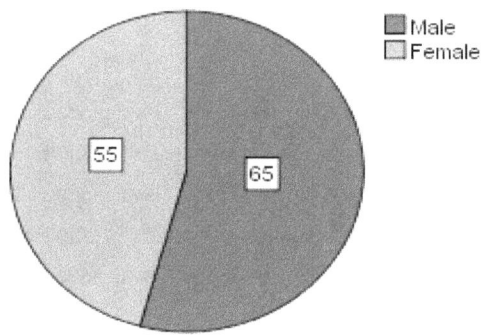

Figure 9 Pie Chart Representation of Students' Gender

The proportion of 120 female and male student respondents who took part in the questionnaire survey is shown in Table 4.11 and Figure 9. There were 65 male and 55 female students that completed the survey. Each group had a proportion of 54.2 % and 45.8%, respectively.

4.3.2 Work Experience

Table 4--12: Frequency of Score of Working Experience, (N=120)

Score	f	Per cent
Yes	108	90.0
No	12	10.0

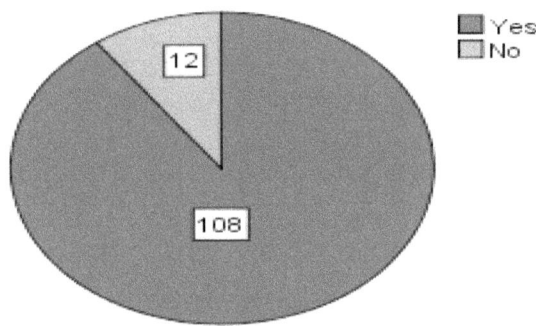

Figure 10 Pie Chart Representation of Working Experience of Students

Table 4.12 and Figure 10 have shown the working experience of the student in the hotel industry. There are 108 students who have experience working in the hotel either during industrial training or vocational training and only 12 students said that they did not have any industry experience. Almost 90% of respondents are having industrial experience and only 10 per cent respondents do not have any industry experience.

4.3.3 Year of Study

Table 4--13: Frequency of Score of Year of Study, (N=120)

Score	f	Per cent
2nd Year	23	19.2
3rd Year	36	30.0
4th Year	61	50.8

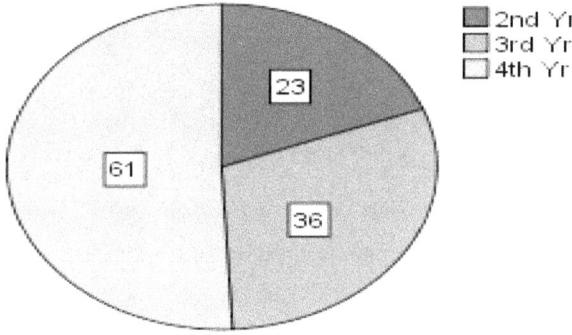

Figure 11 Pie Chart Representation of Year of Study

Table 4.13 and Figure 11 inform about the year of study in the hotel management program. 23 students who took part in the survey was from their 2nd year of study, 36 students were from the 3rd year and 61 students were from the final year of their studies. In per centage, 19.2%, 30.0% and 50.8% respectively.

4.3.4 Willingness To Work in Industry

Table 4--14: Frequency of Score of Willingness to Work, (N=120)

Score	f	Per cent
Male	96	80.0
Female	24	20.0

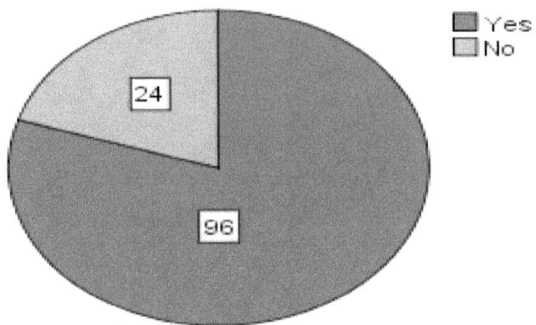

Figure 12 Pie Chart Representation of Students' Willingness to Work

Table 4.14 and Figure 12 talk about the students' willingness to work in the industry. 96 respondents were positive to join the hotel industry with 80% and only 24 respondents were not interested to join the hotel industry with 20%.

4.4 Central Tendencies Measurement of Constructs

SPSS version 22.0 will be used in this section. To compute the mean of our variables, we'll create a frequency table. The standard deviation for each of the statements examined in our questionnaire will also be provided in this section. The frequency of each statement on the Likert scale will be determined using the data collected from our respondents, which will be converted into per centages. The mean and standard deviation of the statements will be tallied in table form in this section.

Table 4--15: Central Tendency of Job Satisfaction

Items	SD	D	N	A	SA	Mean	SD	Mean Rank
1. You enjoy your work.	21	66	142	97	6	3.00	0.90	7
2. You have reasonable work load.	10	71	185	23	43	3.05	0.96	5
3. You get salary on time.	6	67	144	80	35	3.21	0.95	1
4. You are able to full fill family requirements.	32	64	88	137	11	3.09	1.06	4
5. You get promotion opportunities.	6	73	189	35	29	3.02	0.87	6
6. You have effective leadership at workplace.	11	70	143	68	40	3.17	1.00	2
7. You get appreciation for your contribution.	9	108	62	138	15	3.13	1.01	3

*SD-Strongly Disagree, D-Disagree, N-Neutral, A-Agree, SA-Strongly Agree

The central tendency assessment of work satisfaction components is depicted in the table above. On a Likert scale, values range from (1) strongly disagree to (5) strongly agree for this trait.

The statement 'You get your salary on time' had the highest mean of 3.21 when compared to the other statements. 6.3 per cent of 332 respondents strongly disagree with this statement, 19.9 per cent disagree with this statement, 42.8 per cent remain neutral on this statement, 29.2 per cent agree with this statement, and 1.8 per cent strongly agree with this statement.

Secondly, with a mean of 3.17, the statement 'You have an effective leadership at workplace' received the second-highest score. This statement is strongly disagreed with by 3.3 per cent of all responders. This remark is disagreed by 21.1 per cent of respondents, neutral by 43.1 per cent, agreed by 20.5 per cent, and strongly agreed by 12 per cent.

Among the other statements in this category, the statement 'You gain an appreciation for your work' received the third-highest mean score of 3.13. 5.2 per cent of 332 respondents strongly disagree with this statement, 2.7 per cent strongly disagree with this statement, 32.5 per cent strongly disagree with this statement, 18.7% of respondents are neutral, 41.6 per cent agree, and 4.5 per cent strongly agree with this statement, while 18.7% of respondents are neutral, 41.6 per cent agree, and 4.5 per cent strongly agree with this statement.

The statement 'You are able to fulfil family requirements' has the fourth-highest mean score of 3.09 among these statements. 9.6 per cent of total respondents strongly disagree with this statement, 19.3 per cent disagree with this statement, 26.3 per cent are neutral with this statement, 41.3 per cent agree with this statement, and 3.3 per cent strongly agree with this statement.

The statement 'You have a reasonable workload' has the seventh-highest average score of 3.05. Total 3 per cent of 332 respondents strongly disagree with this statement, 21.4 per cent disagree with this statement, 55.7 per cent have a neutral opinion on this statement, 6.9% agree with this statement, and 13.0 per cent strongly agree with this statement.

In this variable, the statement with the sixth mean score, 3.02, is 'You get promotion opportunities.' There is 1.8 per cent of respondents who strongly disagree with this statement, 22.0 per cent of respondents who disagree with this statement, 56.9% of respondents who are neutral, 10.5 per cent of respondents who agree with this statement, and 8.7% of respondents who strongly agree with this statement.

The statement 'You enjoy your work' has the seventh-highest mean score with a mean value of 3.00. Total 6.3 per cent of respondents strongly disagree with this statement, 19.9% disagree with this statement, 42.8 per cent have a neutral opinion on this statement, 29.2 per cent agree with this statement, and 1.8 per cent strongly agree with this statement.

Table 4--16: Central Tendency of Employees' Benefits

Items	SD	D	N	A	SA	Mean	SD	Mean Rank
1. You get housing facility or HRA.	45	85	120	74	8	2.74	1.03	4
2. You have child care policy in company.	7	123	159	38	5	2.73	0.75	5
3. Hotel provides transport facility.	7	102	171	43	9	2.83	0.78	2
4. Hotel provides health insurance.	22	103	81	118	8	2.96	1.01	1
5. You get incentives and bonus.	14	101	179	30	8	2.75	0.77	3
6. Hotel provide free on the job meal.	9	124	112	87	0	2.83	0.85	2

*SD-Strongly Disagree, D-Disagree, N-Neutral, A-Agree, SA-Strongly Agree

The central tendency measurement of employee benefit components is depicted in the table above. This trait is also assessed using a Likert scale, with values ranging from (1) strongly disagree to (5) strongly agree.

When compared to the other statements, the statement "you get housing facility or HRA." had the highest mean of 1.03. Of the 332 respondents, 13.6 per cent strongly disagree with this statement, 25.6 per cent disagree with this statement, 36.1 per cent remain neutral, 22.3 per cent agree with this statement, and 2.4 per cent strongly agree with this statement.

Second, the statement "hotel provides health insurance" earned the second-highest score, with a mean of 1.01. 6.6 per cent of all respondents strongly disagree with this assertion. This comment is disagreed by 31% of respondents, neutral by 24.4 %, agreed by 35.5 %, and highly agreed by 2.4 %.

Among the statements in this variable, the statement 'hotel provides free on-the-job meal' had the third-highest mean score of 0.85. There is 2.7 per cent of 332 respondents who strongly disagree with this statement, 37.3 per cent who disagree with this statement, 33.7 per cent who are indifferent with this statement, 26.2 per cent who agree but no one strongly agrees with this statement.

The statement 'hotel provides transportation facilities' has the fourth-highest mean score of 0.78 among these statements. There is 2.1 per cent of total respondents who choose strongly disagree as to their opinion on this statement, 30.7 per cent who disagree with this statement, 51.5 per cent who are neutral with this statement, 13 per cent who agree with this statement, and 2.7 per cent who strongly agree with this statement.

Out of all of these statements, the statement 'you get incentives and bonuses' gets the fifth-highest mean score of 0.77. There are 4.2 per cent respondents are strongly disagree with this statement, 30.4 per cent disagree with this statement, 53.9 per cent have a moderate opinion on this statement, 9 per cent agree with this statement, and 2.4 per cent strongly agree with this statement, out of the 332 respondents.

At this variable, the statement with the sixth-highest mean score, 0.75, is 'you have a child care policy in your company.' There is 2.1 per cent of respondents who severely disagree with this statement, 37 per cent who disagree with this statement, 47.9 per cent who are neutral with this statement, 11.4 per cent who agree with this statement, and 1.5 per cent who strongly agree with this statement.

Table 4--17: Central Tendency of Training & Development

Items	SD	D	N	A	SA	Mean	SD	Mean Rank
1. Hotel provide training opportunities.	13	131	146	42	0	2.65	0.75	6
2. Hotel organize training program to enhance employee competencies.	25	123	146	31	7	2.61	0.84	3
3. Hotel provides different kinds of training.	45	109	137	36	5	2.54	0.91	2
4. Frequency of providing training programs are sufficient for your growth.	42	90	149	46	5	2.64	0.92	1
5. Hotel has provision for on-off the job training.	24	121	148	34	5	2.62	0.82	4
6. Hotel emphasize long term development for employees.	14	128	146	44	0	2.66	0.76	5

*SD-Strongly Disagree, D-Disagree, N-Neutral, A-Agree, SA-Strongly Agree

The statement "Frequency of providing training program are sufficient for your growth" got the highest mean of 0.92 when compared to the other statements. There is 12.7 per cent of 332 respondents who strongly disagree with this statement, 27.1% who disagree with this statement, 44.9 per cent who remain neutral on this statement, 13.9 per cent who agree with this statement, and 1.5 per cent who strongly agree with this statement.

Second, the statement 'hotel provides different kinds of training' earned the second-highest score, with a mean of 0.91. Total 13.6 per cent of all respondents strongly disagree with this assertion. This comment is disagreed by 32.8% of respondents, neutral by 41.3 %, agreed by 10.8 %, and highly agreed by 1.5 %.

Among the statements in this variable, the statement 'hotel organizes training program to enhance employee competencies' had the third-highest mean score of 0.84. There is 7.5 per cent of 332 respondents who strongly disagree with this statement, 37 per cent who disagree with this statement, 44 per cent are neutral with this statement, 9.3 per cent agree and 2.1 per cent are strongly agrees with this statement.

Among these claims, the statement 'Hotel has provision for on-off the job training' gets the fourth highest mean score of 0.82. Strongly disagree is chosen by 7.2 per cent of total respondents, followed by 36.4 per cent who disagree, 44.6 per cent who are neutral, 10.2 per cent who agree, and 1.5 per cent who strongly agree with this statement.

Out of all of these claims, the statement 'Hotel emphasizes long-term development for employees' gets the fifth-highest mean score of 0.76. 4.2 per cent highly disagree with this statement, 38.6% disagree with this statement, 44 per cent have a neutral opinion on this statement, 13.3% agree with this statement, and none strongly agree with this statement among the 332 responses.

The statement with the sixth-highest mean score, 0.75, in this category is 'Hotels provide training opportunities.' There is 3.9 per cent of respondents who strongly disagree with this statement, 39.5 per cent disagree with it, 44 per cent are neutral about it, 12.7 per cent agree with it, and no one strongly agrees with it.

Table 4--18: Central Tendency of Employee's Perception

Items	SD	D	N	A	SA	Mean	SD	Mean Rank
1. You feel motivated in your job.	25	82	139	70	0	2.91	0.97	6
2. You feel to put extra efforts for organizational goals.	33	72	153	54	20	2.87	1.00	4
3. You feel internal connection with your organization.	35	98	140	42	17	2.72	0.99	5
4. You are looking for job change.	38	80	120	74	20	2.87	1.07	1
5. You feel working environment is positive in organization.	37	77	138	66	14	2.83	1.01	3
6. You feel behaviour of top management is good with employees.	51	67	144	54	16	2.75	1.05	2

*SD-Strongly Disagree, D-Disagree, N-Neutral, A-Agree, SA-Strongly Agree

When compared to the other statements, the statement 'You are looking for a job change' had the highest mean of 1.07. Of the 332 respondents, 11.4 per cent highly disagree with this statement, 24.1 per cent disagree with this statement, 36.1 per cent remain neutral, 22.3 per cent agree with this statement, and 6% strongly agree with this statement.

Second, the statement 'You feel behaviour of top management is good with employees' earned the second-highest score, with a mean of 1.05. A total of 15.4 per cent of all respondents strongly disagree with this assertion. This comment is disagreed by 20.2 per cent of respondents, neutral by 43.4 per cent, agreed by 16.3 per cent, and highly agreed by 4.8 per cent.

Among the statements in this variable, the statement 'You feel working environment is positive in organization' had the third-highest mean score of 1.01. There is 11.1 per cent of 332 respondents who strongly disagree with this statement, 24.1 per cent who disagree with this statement, 36.1 per cent who are neutral with this statement, 22.3 per cent who agree and 6 per cent are strongly agrees with this statement.

Among these assertions, the statement 'You feel to put extra efforts for organisational goals' gets the fourth highest mean score of 1.00. There are 9.9% of total respondents who strongly disagree with this statement, 21.7 per cent who disagree with it, 46.1 per cent who are indifferent about it, 21.1 per cent who agree with it, and no one who strongly agrees with it.

Out of all of these claims, the statement 'You feel internal connection with your organisation' has the fifth-highest mean score of 0.99. Total 10.5 per cent highly disagree with this statement, 29.5 per cent disagree with this statement, 42.2 per cent are neutral on this statement, 12.7 per cent agree with this statement, and 5.1 per cent strongly agree with this statement, out of 332 respondents.

The statement with the sixth-highest means score, 0.75, in this variable is 'You feel motivated in your job.' 7.5 per cent of respondents strongly disagree with this statement, 24.7 per cent disagree with this statement, 41.9 per cent are indifferent, 21.1 per cent agree with this statement, and no one strongly agrees with this statement.

Table 4--19: Central Tendency of Career Choice

Items	SD	D	N	A	SA	Mean	SD	Mean Rank
1. You feel satisfy with your career.	23	120	119	57	13	2.75	0.95	6
2. You feel other career options are comparatively good.	33	83	145	60	11	2.80	0.96	5
3. You feel proud to work in industry.	52	102	127	38	13	2.57	1.01	4
4. Society respects you as hotel professional.	36	127	76	80	13	2.72	1.07	2
5. Hotel industry is good for career progression.	51	86	127	58	10	2.67	1.03	3
6. Hotel industry is equally good for male and female.	70	88	119	42	13	2.52	1.08	1

*SD-Strongly Disagree, D-Disagree, N-Neutral, A-Agree, SA-Strongly Agree

The statement 'Hotel industry is equally good for male and female' got the highest mean of 1.08 when compared to the other statements. There is 21.1 per cent of 332 respondents who strongly disagree with this statement, 26.5 per cent who disagree with this statement, 35.8 per cent who remain neutral on this statement, 12.7 per cent who agree with this statement, and 3.9 per cent who strongly agree with this statement.

Second, the statement 'Society respects you as hotel professional' earned the second-highest score, with a mean of 1.07. A total of 10.8 per cent of all respondents strongly disagree with this assertion. This comment is disagreed by 38.3 per cent of respondents, neutral by 22.9 per cent, agreed by 24.1 per cent, and highly agreed by 3.9 per cent.

Among the statements in this variable, the statement 'Hotel industry is good for career progression' had the third-highest mean score of 1.03. There is 15.4 per cent of 332 respondents who strongly disagree with this statement, 25.9 per cent who disagree with this statement, 38.3 per cent who are neutral with this statement, 17.5 per cent who agree and only 3.0 per cent are strongly agreed with this statement.

Among these assertions, the statement 'You feel proud to work in industry' gets the fourth highest mean score of 1.01. 15.7 per cent of total respondents strongly disagree with this statement, 30.7 per cent disagree with this statement, 38.3 per cent are indifferent with this statement, 11.4 per cent agree with this statement, and no one disagrees with this statement. This remark is supported by 3.9 per cent of those who strongly agree with it.

The statement 'You feel other career options are comparatively good' has the fifth-highest mean score of 0.96 out of all of these statements. Among the 332 respondents, 9.9 per cent strongly disagree with this statement, 25 per cent disagree with this statement, 43.7 per cent have a neutral opinion on this statement, while 18.1 per cent agree with this statement and 3.3 per cent are strongly agree with this statement.

'You feel satisfy with your career' has the sixth-highest mean score of 0.95 in this variable. 6.9% severely disagree with this statement, 36.1 per cent disagree with this statement, 35.8% are indifferent with this statement, 17.2 per cent agree with this statement, and 3.9 per cent strongly agree with this statement, according to the survey.

Table 4--20: Central Tendency of Interns-Students

Factors	SD	D	N	A	SA	Mean	SD	Mean Rank
1. A job where I gain transferable skills	4	27	36	38	15	3.28	1.05	3
2. A job that is respected	0	35	54	16	15	3.09	0.96	7
3. Reasonable workload	9	20	40	36	15	3.23	1.11	4
4. A job with high quality resources and equipment	12	19	38	23	28	3.30	1.27	2
5. The opportunity to travel abroad	9	19	42	22	28	3.34	1.21	1
6. Job mobility ease to get job anywhere	13	25	23	31	28	3.30	1.33	2
7. Good starting salary	0	28	53	24	15	3.22	0.95	5
8. A job where i can use university degree	6	22	60	32	0	2.98	0.81	10
9. A job, I will find enjoyable	14	19	65	18	4	2.83	0.94	11
10. Colleagues that I can get along	8	17	67	21	7	3.02	0.91	9
11. A job gives me responsibility	19	13	62	26	0	2.79	0.96	12
12. A secure job	16	24	34	33	13	3.03	1.21	8
13. A career, provides intellectual challenges	9	32	27	38	14	3.13	1.16	6

*SD-Strongly Disagree, D-Disagree, N-Neutral, A-Agree, SA-Strongly Agree

When compared to the other statements, Statement "The opportunity to travel abroad" has the highest mean value 3.34, as shown in Table 29. 3.3 per cent of 120 respondents strongly disagree with this statement, 22.5 per cent disagree with this statement, 30% remain neutral, 31.7 per cent agree with this statement, and 12.5 per cent strongly agree with this statement.

The second statement 'Job mobility ease to get a job anywhere and 'A job with high-quality resources and equipment are having the second highest mean value 3.30. For the statement job mobility ease to get a job anywhere, there are 10.8 per cent respondents are strongly disagreed, 20.8 per cent have disagreed, 19.2 per cent respondents are neutral while 25.8 per cent are agreed with the statement and only 12.5 per cent respondents strongly agree with the statement. While on other hand next statement is a job with high-quality resources and equipment with the same mean score. There is 10 per cent of respondents out of 120 who strongly disagree with the statement, 15.8 per cent have disagreed, 31.7 per cent do not have any opinion and became neutral. 19.2 per cent of respondents do agree with the statement and 23.3 per cent are strongly agree.

Among the statements in this variable, the statement 'A job where I gain transferable skills' had the third-highest mean score of 3.28. There is 3.3 per cent of 120 respondents who strongly disagree with this statement, 22.5 per cent who disagree with this statement, 30.0 per cent who are neutral with this statement, 31.7 per cent who agree and only 12.5 per cent are strongly agrees with this statement.

The statement '3. Reasonable workload' has the fourth-highest mean score of 3.23 among these statements. There is 7.5 per cent of total respondents who choose strongly disagree as to their opinion on this statement, 16.7 per cent who disagree with this statement, 33.3 per cent who are neutral with this statement, 30.0 per cent who agree with this statement, and no one is there 12.5 per cent who strongly agree with this statement.

The statement 'Good starting salary' has the fifth-highest mean score of 3.22 out of all of these statements. Among the 120 respondents, no one strongly disagreed with this statement but 23.3 per cent disagreed with this statement, 44.2 per cent have a neutral opinion on this statement, while 21.0 per cent agree with this statement and 12.5 per cent are strongly agree with this statement.

At this variable, the statement with the sixth-highest mean score, 3.13, is 'A career, provides intellectual challenges.' There are 7.5 per cent of respondents who strongly disagree with this statement, 26.7 per cent who disagree with this statement, 22.5 per cent who are neutral with this statement, 31.7 per cent who agree with this statement, and 11.7 per cent respondents who strongly agree with this statement.

Another statement 'A job that is respected' is having the seventh-highest mean value with 3.09. Out of the total of 120 student-interns, no one strongly disagree with the statement, 29.2 per cent have disagreed and 45 per cent preferred to be neutral. 13.3 and 12.5 per cent of respondents are agreed and strongly agree with the statement.

The statement 'A secure job' is a statement which is having the eighth highest mean value with 3.03. 13.3 per cent of respondents strongly disagree with the statement, 20.0 per cent have disagreed and 28.3 per cent preferred to be neutral. 27.5 and 10.8 per cent of respondents are agreed and strongly agree with the statement.

The statement 'Colleagues that I can get along ' has the ninth highest mean score of 3.02 out of all of these statements. Among the 120 respondents, 6.7 per cent are strongly disagreed with this statement but 14.2 per cent disagreed with this statement, 55.8 per cent have a neutral opinion on this statement, while 17.5 per cent agree with this statement and 5.8 per cent are strongly agree with this statement

The statement 'A job where I can use university degree' has the tenth highest mean score of 2.98 out of all of these statements. Among the 120 respondents, 5.0 per cent are strongly disagreed with this statement but 18.3 per cent disagreed with this statement, 50.0 per cent have a neutral opinion on this statement, while 26.7 per cent agreed with this statement and no one is strongly agreed with this statement.

At this variable, the statement with the eleventh highest mean score, 2.83, is 'A job, I will find enjoyable.' There is 11.7 per cent of respondents who strongly disagree with this statement, 15.8 per cent who disagree with this statement, 54.2 per cent who are neutral with this statement, 15 per cent who agree with this statement, and 3.3 per cent respondents who strongly agree with this statement.

The statement 'A job gives me responsibility is having a mean value of 2.79 and stands at a twelfth stand. There is 15.8 per cent of respondents who strongly disagree with this statement, 10.8 per cent who disagree with this statement, 51.7 per cent who are neutral with this statement, 21.7 per cent who agree with this statement, and no respondent strongly agrees with this statement.

4.5 Scale Measurement

The validity and reliability of the study instrument were assessed using exploratory factor analysis and Cronbach's Alpha. We also assessed the data normality to choose the most relevant parametric and non-parametric tests.

4.5.1 Internal Reliability Test

Table 4--21: Cronbach's Alpha Reliability Analysis

Construct	Coefficient Alpha Value	No. of Items
Job Satisfaction	0.932	7
Employee Benefits	0.908	6
Training and Development	0.958	6
Employee Perception	0.938	6
Career Choice	0.956	6

Source: Developed for the research

Coefficient Alpha was used in the study to assess the reliability of the questionnaire. As stated in Chapter 3, an alpha value of 0.80 to 0.95 is regarded as very excellent reliability; a value of 0.70 to 0.80 is considered good reliability. When the alpha value is between 0.60 and 0.70, it is deemed acceptable dependability, and when it is less than 0.60, it is called poor reliability.

According to the table above, the coefficient alpha value of job satisfaction is 0.932, which is regarded to be very good reliability. Furthermore, the result reveals that the training and development variable has the highest value, 0.958, which is regarded to be extremely excellent reliability.

Employee benefits and employee perception are likewise regarded to have incredibly high reliability because their coefficient alpha values are 0.908 and 0.938, respectively. Aside from that, career choice has a very high level of reliability, with a coefficient alpha value of 0.956.

Overall, the internal reliability test results suggest that all variables in this study are consistent and reliable, as the coefficient alpha value of all constructs falls between

0.80 and 0.95. As a consequence, the results of this questionnaire are eligible for future investigation.

4.5.2 Test of Data Normality

Asymmetry and kurtosis values between -2 and +2 are regarded as acceptable for demonstrating a normal univariate distribution (George & Mallery, 2010). Data is considered normal if the skewness is between 2 and +2 and the kurtosis is between 7 and +7, according to (Hair et al. 2010) and (Bryne, 2010). Furthermore, Wiederman, Hagmann, and von Eye (2015) provide an easy-to-use z-test for comparing variable skewness.

4.5.2.1 Normality test using skewness and kurtosis

A z-test is used to test normality using skewness and kurtosis. A z-score can be calculated by dividing the skew or excess kurtosis values by their standard errors.

$$Z = \frac{\text{Skew value}}{SE_{skewness}}, \quad Z = \frac{\text{Excess kurtosis}}{SE_{excess\ kurtosis}}$$

Table 4--22: Descriptive Statistics of mean score of factors

Factors	N	Mean	SD	Median	Min	Max	Skewness	SE	Kurtosis	SE
Job Satisfaction	332	3.10	0.81	3.14	1.43	4.71	-.07	.13	-.66	.27
Employee Benefits	332	2.81	0.72	2.83	1.33	4.50	.05	.13	-.67	.27
Training & Development	332	2.62	0.73	2.67	1.33	4.67	.17	.13	-.31	.27
Employee Perception	332	2.83	0.89	3.00	1.17	4.67	-.06	.13	-.62	.27
Career Choice	332	2.67	0.92	2.67	1.00	4.67	.18	.13	-.61	.27

As table 4.22 and figure 13 shows the mean score of factor job satisfaction total number of respondents N=332 with the mean value of 3.10 and the standard deviation is 0.81. The table also shows a minimum value of 1.43 and a maximum value of 4.71. The table represents the median with 3.14 of job satisfaction. The mean score of job satisfaction has a skewness value of -0.07 with a standard error of 0.13 and the kurtosis value is -0.66 with a standard error of 0.27. The z-value of skewness is -0.53

which is in the range between -2 to + 2 and the z value of kurtosis is -2.44 which is in the range between -7 to +7. So, the data on job satisfaction is normally distributed.

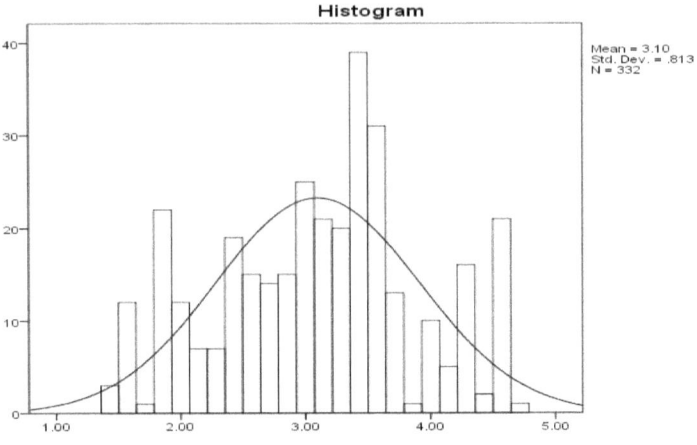

Figure 13 Histogram of Normality Curve-Job Satisfaction

The mean score of the factor employee benefits, total number of respondents (N=332) with a mean value of 2.81 and a standard deviation of 0.72 is shown in table 4.22 and figure 14. The table also shows a minimum value of 1.33 and a maximum value of 4.50. The table depicts the median of employee benefits, which is 2.83. The skewness value of the total mean score of employee benefits is .05 with a standard error of 0.13, and the kurtosis value is -0.67 with a standard error of 0.27. Skewness has a z-value of 0.38, which is in the range of -2 to +2, and kurtosis has a z-value of -2.48, which is in the range of -7 to +7. As a result, employee's benefits data is normally distributed.

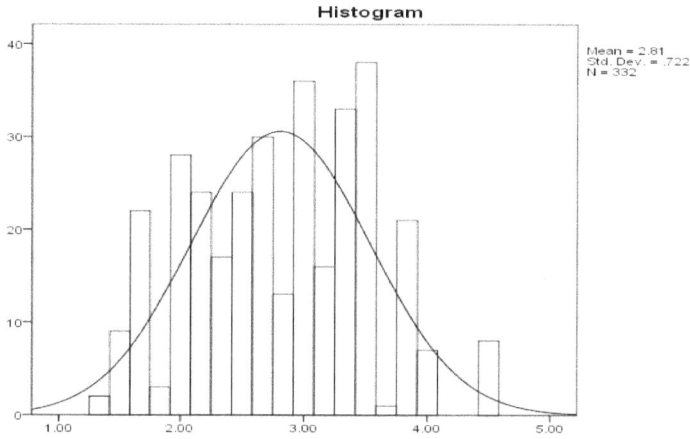

Figure 14 Histogram of Normality Curve-Employee's Benefits

As table 4.22 and figure 15 shows the mean score of the factor training & development, the total number of respondents (N=332) with the mean value of 2.62 and the standard deviation is 0.73. The table also shows a minimum value of 1.33 and a maximum value of 4.67. The table represents the median with 2.67 of training & development. The mean score of training & development has a skewness value of 0.17 with a standard error of 0.13 and the kurtosis value is -0.31 with a standard error of 0.27. The z-value of skewness is 1.30 which is in the range between -2 to + 2 and the z-value of kurtosis is -1.14 which is in the range between -7 to +7. So, the data on training & development is normally distributed.

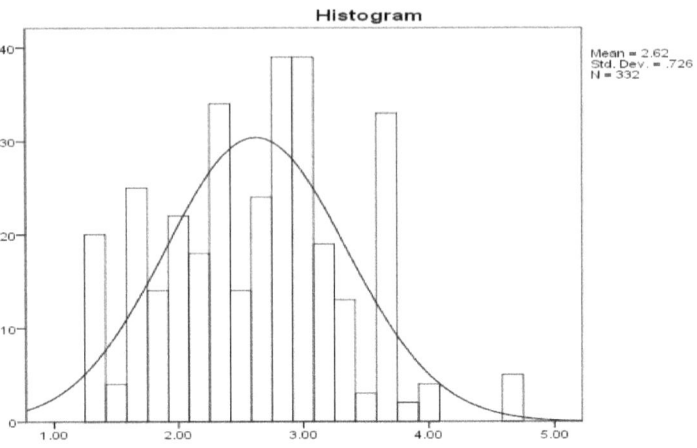

Figure 15 Histogram of Normality Curve-Training & Development

The mean score of the factor employee's perception, the total number of respondents (N=332) with a mean value of 2.83 and a standard deviation of 0.89 is shown in table 4.22 and figure 16. The table also shows a minimum value of 1.17 and a maximum value of 4.67. The table depicts the median of an employee's perception, which is 3.00. The skewness value of the total mean score of employee benefits is negative 0.06 with a standard error of 0.13, and the kurtosis value is negative 0.62 with a standard error of 0.27. Skewness has a z-value of -0.46, which is in the range of -2 to +2, and kurtosis has a z-value of -2.29, which is in the range of -7 to +7. As a result, employee's perception data is normally distributed.

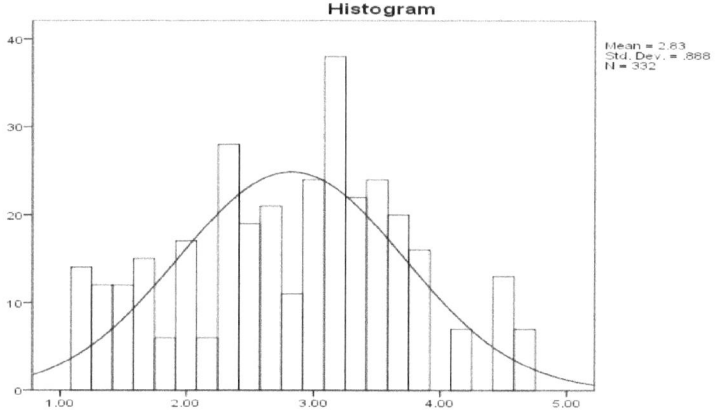

Figure 16 *Histogram of Normality Curve- Employee's Perception*

The mean score of the factor career choice, the total number of respondents (N=332) with a mean value of 2.67 and a standard deviation of 0.92 is shown in table 4.22 and figure 17. The table also shows a minimum value of 1.00 and a maximum value of 4.67. The table depicts the median of career choice, which is 2.67. The skewness value of the total mean score of employee benefits is .18 with a standard error of 0.13, and the kurtosis value is negative 0.61 with a standard error of 0.27. Skewness has a z-value of 1.38, which is in the range of -2 to +2, and kurtosis has a z- value of -2.25, which is in the range of -7 to +7. As a result, career choice data is normally distributed.

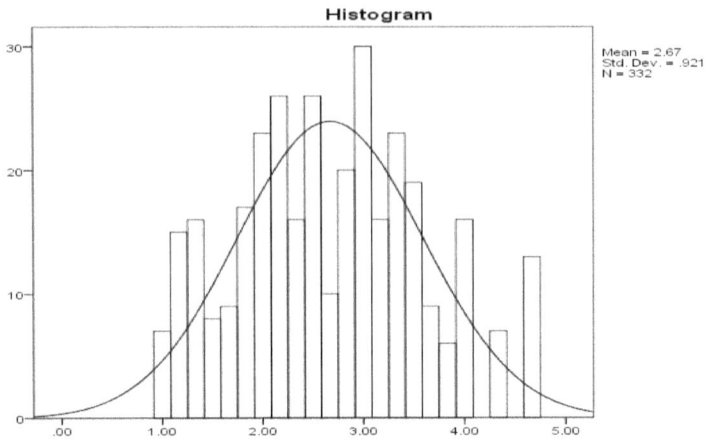

Figure 17 Histogram of Normality Curve- Career Choice

Table 4--23: Descriptive Statistics of mean score of factors (Student Interns)

Factors	N	Mean	SD	Median	Min	Max	Skewness	SD	Kurtosis	SD
Mean score of factors	120	3.12	0.75	3.12	1.62	4.46	-.11	.22	-.95	.44

The mean score of the factor, the total number of respondents (N=120) with a mean value of 3.12 and a standard deviation of 0.7 is shown in table 4.23 and figure 18. The table also shows a minimum value of 1.62 and a maximum value of 4.46. The table depicts the median mean score of student interns, which is 3.12. The skewness value of the mean score is negative.11 with a standard error of 0.22, and the kurtosis value is negative 0.95 with a standard error of 0.44. Skewness has a z-value of -0.5, which is in the range of -2 to +2, and kurtosis has a z- value of -2.15, which is in the range of -7 to +7. As a result, the mean score of student interns' data is normally distributed.

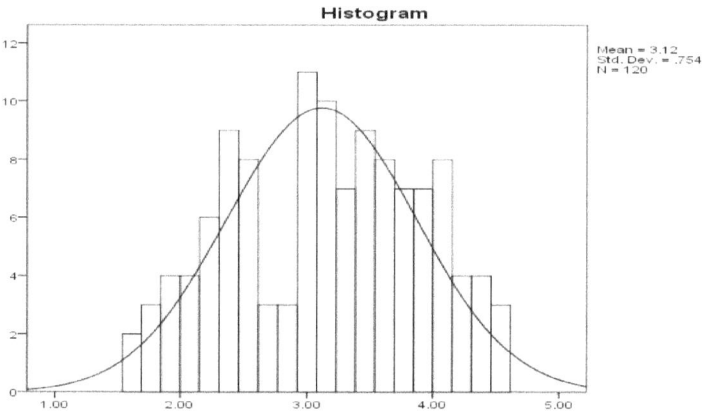

Figure 18 Histogram of Normality Curve- Student Interns

4.6 Factor Analysis

Factor analysis is a method of condensing data from numerous variables into a few variables. As a result, it is also known as "dimension reduction" at times. Our data's "dimensions" have been reduced to five "components or super-variables". As mentioned in chapter 3, our data has been divided into five components which are job satisfaction, Employee' benefits, training & development, employee perception and career choice. We utilised the Principal Component Analysis (PCA) approach using SPSS version 22.

4.6.1 KMO Test and Bartlett's Test of Sphericity to Check Adequacy Of Sample

The Kaiser-Meyer-Olkin sampling adequacy test is used to examine if partial correlations between variables are moderate. The Kaiser-Meyer-Olkin test value should be more than 0.5 (KMO> 0.5) to establish the validity of the used variables. If the correlation matrix is an identity matrix, the factor model is erroneous, according to Bartlett's test of sphericity. For Bartlett's test, the significance level should not exceed 0.05. (Sig. 0.05).

As a result, the validity of the measuring techniques will be addressed for each content construct. The results of each validity test are shown in the tables below.

Table 30 displays the results of the KMO and Bartlett's sphericity tests for the overall construct.

Table 4--24: KMO and Bartlett's Test for overall construct

KMO and Bartlett's Test		
Kaiser-Meyer-Olkin Measure of Sampling Adequacy.		.905
Bartlett's Test of Sphericity	Approx. Chi-Square	9511.03
	df	465.00
	Sig.	.000

The sufficiency and suitability test of data KMO for the execution of factor analysis for overall build demonstrates that the data set is suitable for factor analysis since the obtained number is larger than 0.5. (0.905). Similarly, the number of significant Bartlett's tests equals 0.01 and is less than the significant threshold of 0.05, indicating that the correlation matrix contains important information.

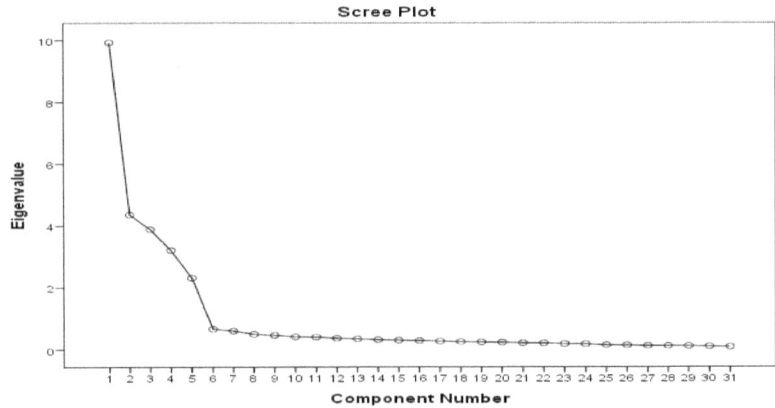

Figure 19 Scree Plot for Overall Construct

Also, the result of the Scree Plot shows that only one factor has an eigenvalue of over 1.00. Figure 19 shows the result of the Scree Plot for Perceived usefulness.

Table 4--25: Total Variance Explained for Overall Construct

Component	Extraction Sums of Squared Loadings		
	Total	% of Variance	Cumulative %
1	9.92	32.01	32.01
2	4.36	14.06	46.07
3	3.89	12.54	58.61
4	3.21	10.37	68.98
5	2.32	7.50	76.48

*Extraction Method: Principal Component Analysis.

Furthermore, the total variance is explained for the overall construct in table 4,25, which shows the loadings of different components which are in the range of 2.32 to 9.92. The per centage of the variance of the first component is 32.01 which mean that this factor is explaining 32 % of the total variance. The second component is having 14.06 which depicts that this factor explains 14% of the total variance. The third component is having 12.54 which shows that about 12% variable explained by this factor. Similarly, the fourth and fifth components are having 10.37 and 7.50 respectively and these also depict that these factors explain 10 per cent and 7 per cent of the total variables.

4.6.2 Confirmatory Factor Analysis – Structural Equation Modelling

Confirmatory factor analysis (CFA) is a statistical method for determining the factor structure of a collection of data. CFA may be used to determine if there is a relationship between observable variables and their hidden components. To check the validity of the questionnaire, we ran a model fit by using confirmatory factor analysis on the AMOS-SEM.

CFA is a sort of factor analysis that may be conducted using the Structure Equation Modelling Approach (SEM). In SEM, all straight arrows from the latent variable are deleted, leaving just the arrow that has to observe the variable indicating the covariance between each pair of latent. The disturbance terms will be allocated to their proper variables, and the straight arrows will be error-free. The factor is regarded as excellent if the standardised error term in SEM is less than the absolute value two; if it is larger than two, there is still some unexplained variation that may be explained by the factor. The Chi-square and other goodness-of-fit indices are used to determine how well the model fits.

As per figure 19, Confirmatory factor analysis shows the estimated loading of standardized regressing weights in the range of 0.70 to 0.90 which will be considered excellent as the value must be greater than 0.30.

Table 4--26: Model Fit Summary

Indices	Standard Value
Comparative Fit Index (CFI)	0.95
Goodness Fit Index (GFI)	0.86
Adjusted Goodness of Fit Index (AGFI)	0.84
Root Mean Square Error of Approximation (RMSEA)	0.06
Normed Fit Index (NFI)	0.91
Chai-Square/ Degree of Freedom (CMIN/DF)	2.10

Table 4.26 depicts the model fit summary of the variables. It shows that the comparative fit index value is 0.95 which is considered good as its value must be equal to or greater than 0.90 as mentioned in chapter three, table 7. The goodness fit index value is 0.86 which is approximately 0.90 is again good. Similarly, the adjusted goodness of fit index value is 0.84 which is very nearby 0.90. The root mean square error of the approximation value is 0.06 which is in range, it must be less than 0.08 so it will consider as good. The normed fit index is 0.91 which is more than 0.90 so it will consider good and in last CMIN/DF value is 2.10 and it must be less than 5.00. So, all values are good and this model is fit to run for further analysis.

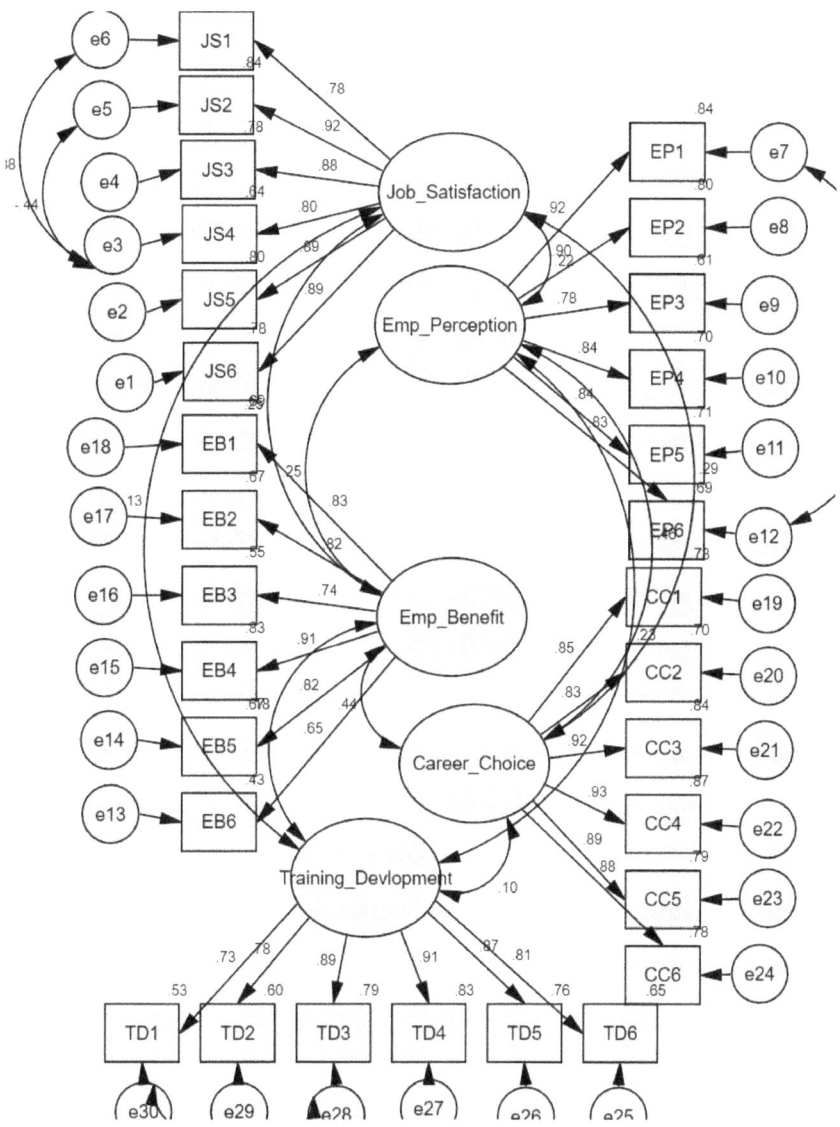

Figure 20 Confirmatory Factor Analysis (First Order)

4.7 Inferential Analyses

4.7.1 Pearson Correlation Coefficient

The Pearson correlation coefficient, according to Zikmund (2003), is a measure of the linear relationship between two metric variables. The degree and direction of a linear relationship between two variables may be determined using Pearson's correlation analysis. It also shows the direction, strength, and significance of all variables in the bivariate relationship of the study.

The values of the Pearson correlation coefficient vary from -1 to +1. A value of +1 indicates that two variables have a positive linear relationship; a value of -1 indicates that two variables have a completely negative linear relationship. A value of 0 indicates that the variables are not connected in a linear way. The coefficient range in the table indicates that the strength of the linear relationship between two variables varies.

Table 4--27: Pearson Correlation Coefficient

Coefficient range	Strength
±0.91 to ±1.0	Very Strong
±0.71 to ±0.90	High
±0.41 to ±0.70	Moderate
±0.21 to ±0.40	Small but definite relationship.
0 to ±0.20	Slight, almost negligible

Source: Hair, J. F. Jr., Money, A. H., Samouel, P., & Page, M. (2007). Research methods for business. Chichester. West Sussex: John Wiley & Sons, Inc.

4.7.1.1 **Hypotheses 1: The relationship between job satisfaction and career choice**

H_0: There is no significant relationship between job satisfaction and career choice in the hotel industry.

H_1: There is a significant relationship between job satisfaction and career choice in the hotel industry.

Table 4--28: Correlation between job satisfaction and career choice

Variable	η	M	SD	1	2
1 Job Satisfaction	332	3.16	.80		
2 Career Choice	332	2.67	.92	0.42**	

**. Correlation is significant at the 0.01 level (2-tailed).

Table 4.28 revealed that job satisfaction has a significant positive correlation with career choice (r=.42, p < 0.01). The value of this correlation coefficient 0.42 is fallen under the coefficient range from ±0.41 to ±0.70. Thus, the relationship between job satisfaction and career choice is moderate. Besides that, the relationship between both of the variables is significant because of the p-value 0.00 is less than the alpha value of 0.01.

As the result, H_0 is rejected and H_1 is accepted, so there is a significant positive relationship between job satisfaction and career choice.

4.7.1.2 Hypotheses 2: The Relationship between Employee' Benefits and career Choice

H_0: There is no significant relation between Employee Benefits and career choice in the hotel industry.

H_1: There is a significant relation between Employee Benefits and career choice in the hotel industry.

Table 4--29: Correlation between employee' benefits and career choice

Variables	η	M	SD	1	2
1. Employee Benefits	332	2.8097	.72251		
2. Career Choice	332	2.6707	.92174	0.44**	

**. Correlation is significant at the 0.01 level (2-tailed).

Table 4.29 revealed that employee' benefits have a significant positive correlation with career choice (r=.44, p < 0.01). The value of this correlation coefficient 0.44 is fallen under the coefficient range from ±0.41 to ±0.70. Thus, the relationship between job satisfaction and career choice is moderate. Besides that, the relationship between both of the variables is significant because of the p-value 0.00 is less than the alpha value of 0.01.

As the result, H_0 is rejected and H_1 is accepted, so there is a significant positive relationship between employee benefits and career choice.

4.7.1.3 Hypotheses 3: The relationship between Training & Development and Career Choice

H_0: There is no significant relation between Training & Development and career choice in the hotel industry.

H_1: There is a significant relation between Training & Development and career choice in the hotel industry.

Table 4--30: Correlation between training & development and career choice

Variables	η	M	SD	1	2
1. Training & Development	332	2.67	0.92		
2. Career Choice	332	2.62	0.73	0.094	

Table 4.30 shows that training & development has a significant positive correlation with career choice (r=.09, p > 0.05). The value of this correlation coefficient 0.09 is fallen under the coefficient range from 0 to ±0.20. Thus, the relationship between training & development and career choice has a slight relation or almost negligible

relation.

As the result, H₀ cannot be rejected and H₁ is rejected, so there is no significant relationship between training & development and career choice.

4.7.1.4 Hypotheses 4: The relationship between Employee' Perception and Career Choice

H_0: There is no significant relationship between employee perception and career choice in the hotel industry.

H_1: There is a significant relationship between employee perception and career choice in the hotel industry.

Table 4-31: Correlation between employee' perception and career choice

Variables	η	M	SD	1	2
1. Employee Perception	332	2.83	0.89		
2. Career Choice	332	2.67	0.92	.44**	

**. Correlation is significant at the 0.01 level (2-tailed).

Table 4.31 revealed that employee' perception has a significant positive correlation with career choice ($r=.44$, $p < 0.01$). The value of this correlation coefficient 0.44 is fallen under the coefficient range from ±0.41 to ±0.70. Thus, the relationship between job satisfaction and career choice is moderate. Besides that, the relationship between both of the variables is significant because of the p-value 0.00 is less than the alpha value of 0.01.

As the result, H₀ is rejected and H₁ is accepted, so there is a significant positive relationship between employee perception and career choice.

4.7.1.5 Hypotheses 5: The relationship among all variables. (Job Satisfaction, Employee's Benefits, Training & Development and Employee's Perception)

H_0: There is no significant relationship among job satisfaction, employee' benefits, training & development and employee' perception.

H_1: There is a significant relation among job satisfaction, employee' benefits, training & development and employee' perception.

Table 4--32: Correlation among all variables

Variables	η	M	SD	1	2	3	4	5
1. Job Satisfaction	332	3.0977	.81306					
2. Employee Benefits	332	2.8092	.72185	0.304**				
3. Training & Development	332	2.6230	.72586	0.124*	0.162**			
4. Employee Perception	332	2.8253	.88767	0.256**	0.265**	0.199**		
5. Career Choice	332	2.6712	.92123	0.365**	0.439**	0.94	0.441**	

*p <0.05, **p<0.01

Table 37 revealed that job satisfaction has significant positive correlation with employee' benefits (r=.30, p < 0.01), training & development (r= .12, p < .05) and employee' perception (r=.26, p < 0.01). It shows that job satisfaction is having a significant small correlation with employee benefit, a slightly positive correlation with training & development and again a small positive correlation with employee' perception.

Employee' benefit is also having a significant positive relationship with training & development (r=.16, p < 0.01) and with employee' perception (r=.26, p<0.01), that shows employee' benefit have an almost negligible correlation with training & development as it falls under 0 to ±0.20 and similarly employee' benefit have a significant small positive relation with employee perception as it falls under the range ±0.21 to ±0.40.

Similarly, training & development is also having a small significant relation with employee' perception (r= .20, p < 0.01). it shows that there is almost a 20 per cent relation between these two variables and falls under the range between 0 to ±0.20 as per table 32.

4.7.2 Multiple Regression Analyses

4.7.2.1 Hypotheses 6: The relationship between four independent variables and Career Choice

H_0: The four independent variables (job satisfaction, employee' benefit, training & development and employee perception) do not have a significant relationship with career choice.

H_1: The four independent variables (job satisfaction, employee' benefit, training & development and employee perception) have a significant relationship with career choice.

Table 4--33: Regression Coefficient of JS, EB, TD and EP on Career Choice

Variables	B	SE	t	P	95%CI
Constant	0.11	0.24	0.45	0.656	(-36,.58)
Job Satisfaction	0.22	0.054	4.09	0.000	(.12,.33)
Employee Benefits	0.38	0.062	6.22	0.000	(.26,.51)
Training & Development	-0.05	0.059	-0.92	0.361	(-.17,.06)
Employee Perception	0.33	0.05	6.64	0	(.23,.43)

*JS-Job Satisfaction, EB-Employee Benefits, TD-Training & Development, EP-Employee Perception

Table 4.33, shows the impact of job satisfaction, employee' benefits, training & development and employee's perception on career choice. The R^2 value of .34 revealed that the predictors explained 34% variance in the outcome variable with $F(4,327) = 42.18$, $p<.00$.

Table 4.34 shows that the R-value is 0.58. The R-value is the correlation coefficient between the dependent variable and the independent variables taken together. The result shows that there is a positive and moderate correlation between the dependent variable (career choice) and independent variables (job satisfaction, employee' benefit, training and development and employee' perception).

The R square indicates the extent to the independent variables can explain the variations in the dependent variable. From this study, the coefficient of determination (R square) is 0.34, which indicated that independent variables (job satisfaction, employee' benefit, training and development and employee' perception) can explain 34% of the variations independent variable (career choice).

Table 4--34: Model Summary

Model	R	R Square	Adjusted R Square	Std. Error of the Estimate
1	.583[a]	.340	.332	.75277

a. Predictors: (Constant), EP, TD, JS, EB

The findings revealed that all independent variables were positively predicted except training & development. The values of standardized coefficients beta (β) value are for job satisfaction, employee benefit, employee perception is (β=.20, p<.00, β=.30, p<.001, β=.32, p<.000) and training & development standardized coefficient beta (β) value is (β =-.04, p>.05), whereas training & development has a negative and non-significant impact on career choice rest all 3 independent variables have a positive and significant impact on career choice.

4.8 Variables Affecting Employee' Perceptions Toward the Hospitality Industry as a Career Choice

This part measures the relationship between several variables that may have effects on

Current employees' perceptions and attitudes toward the industry and their career in the industry. These contingency variables are (1) gender, (2) type of employment and (3) willingness to work in the hotel industry.

Table 4--35: Variables affecting employee' perceptions toward the Hospitality Industry as a career choice

Variable		Mean	SD	T	Sig
Gender	Male	2.60	.95	-1.45	0.149
	Female	2.74	.88		
Type of Employment	Contractual	2.15	.71	-5.64	0.000
	Permanent	2.77	.92		
Willingness to work	Yes	3.16	.74	16.07	0.000
	No	1.93	.63		

Gender

As table 4.35 indicates, an independent-sample t-test was conducted to examine if significant differences were found between respondents' perceptions of hospitality careers according to gender. The results show that female employees tend to have less favourable perceptions ($\bar{\chi}=2.74$) than male students ($\bar{\chi}=2.60$) but, generally, there was no significant gender-based difference in the perception of students toward the hospitality careers.

Type of Employment

Tests were also conducted to examine if there were statistically significant correlations between the respondents' employment type (Permanent or Contractual Employees) and their perceptions of the industry as a career choice. Employees who are working on a contractual basis in the hotel are having a slightly positive perception about a career in the hotel industry with the mean value of (($\bar{\chi}=2.15$) in comparison to those employees who are permanent employees and on the payroll of the hotel ($\bar{\chi}=2.77$). Although, the difference in perception about a career in the hotel industry is not significant between both.

Willingness to Work

Referring again to table 4.35, the test indicated that the mean value of the perceptions of respondents who were willing to work in the hotel industry ($\bar{\chi}=3.16$) is much less than those who are not willing to work in the industry ($\bar{\chi}=1.93$). It shows that employees who are working in the industry are not satisfied with the job in the hotel industry and have a negative or not much positive perception about a career in the industry.

Table 4--36: Variables Affecting Intern-Students' Perceptions toward the Hospitality

Variable		Mean	SD	T	Sig (2 Tailed)
Gender					
	Male	3.21	0.751	1.491	0.139
	Female	3.00	0.748		
Work Experience					
	Yes	3.08	0.75	-1.55	0.124
	No	3.43	0.72		
Willingness to work					
	Yes	3.06	0.766	-1.55	0.124
	No	3.33	0.673		

Gender

As table 4.36 indicates, an independent-sample t-test was conducted to examine if significant differences were found between respondents' perceptions of hospitality careers according to gender. The results show that male employees tend to have less favourable perceptions ($\bar{\chi}=3.21$) than female students ($\bar{\chi}=3.00$) but, generally, there was no significant gender-based difference in the perception of students toward the hospitality careers.

Work Experience

Tests were also conducted to examine if there were statistically significant correlations between the respondents' work experience, whether respondents have exposure to industry or do not have any industry experience. Their perceptions of the industry as a career choice, intern-students who have worked in the hotel as interns are having a slightly positive perception about a career in the hotel industry with the mean value of (($\bar{\chi}=3.08$) in comparison of those who did not experience industry as interns ($\bar{\chi}=3.43$). Although, the difference in perception about a career in the hotel industry is not significant between both.

Willingness to Work

Referring again to table 45, the test indicated that the mean value of the perceptions of respondents who were willing to work in the hotel industry ($\bar{\chi}=3.06$) is more favourable in comparison to those who are not willing to work in the industry ($\bar{\chi}=3.33$). It shows that students as interns who want to pursue their career in the hotel industry and those who do not want to pursue their career in the hotel industry do not have much significant difference.

Table 4-37: Variables Affecting Students' Perceptions toward the Hospitality (ANOVA)

Variable	Mean	SD	F (2,117)	Sig (2 Tailed)	η^2	Post-Hoc
Year of Study						
2nd Year	3.16	0.84				
3rd Year	3.35	0.65	3.28	0.04	0.053	2>1>3
4th Year	2.95	0.74				

Year of Study

Table 4.37 shows mean, standard deviation and F-value for career choice across the year of study groups. Results indicated a significant mean difference across the year of a study group on career choice with $F(2,117) = 3.28$, $p < 0.05$. Findings revealed that senior students (final year) are more likely to have a positive perception towards the industry ($\bar{\chi}=2.95$), followed by 2nd-year students ($\bar{\chi}=3.16$) than 3rd-year students ($\bar{\chi}=3.35$). In other words, as the respondents progress in their degree, their perceptions of the industry improved. The value was 0.05 (< -.50) which indicated a very small effect or negligible effect size. The Post-Hoc comparison indicated significant between-group mean differences of each group with the other two groups.

4.9 Conclusion

Various types of analysis are performed on the data obtained through the survey in this section. First, we ran these data through a demographic analysis. A respondent demographic profile is created as part of this study to determine the demographic characteristics of the respondents.

The use of frequency analysis to get the mean of data gathered is also used in this study to assess the central tendencies of constructs. In the scale measurement step, a reliability study is performed to ensure that the result is reliable.

We used "Principal Component Analysis and Confirmatory Component Analysis" to conduct factor analysis. The principal component analysis is used to reduce a large number of individual items into a smaller number of dimensions, whereas confirmatory factor analysis is used to see if the data fits a measurement model that has been hypothesized. Finally, inferential analyses are used to see if there is a relationship between the independent and dependent variables. To see if the relationship between these variables is significant, the Pearson Correlation Coefficient and Multiple Regression Analysis are used.

We also used the Independent Samples T-test and ANOVA to compare the means of two independent groups in order to see if there is statistical evidence that the associated population means are significantly different, and ANOVA to see how your different groups respond, with a null hypothesis that the groups' means are equal.

The findings of the study will be addressed in further depth in Chapter 5.

Chapter-V

5 SUMMARY OF RESULTS

5.1 Introduction

This chapter will summarize the result and implications from the previous chapter. The format of this chapter starts with a general review of statistical analyses, which includes both descriptive and inferential studies. The key findings will then be discussed, as well as the study's ramifications. The study's shortcomings, as well as suggestions for further research and findings, are discussed.

5.2 Summary of Statistical Analyses

5.2.1 Summary of Descriptive Analyses

The following is a summary explanation of descriptive analysis based on the questionnaire survey results. The demographic profile of responders is described in this descriptive study. To begin, we know that the respondents are divided into two genders:

The 174 questionnaires we obtained through the study included 52.3 per cent male replies and 158 female responses, accounting for 46.6 per cent of the overall population. Because our respondents are fairly evenly divided across gender categories, we have the advantage of being able to defend our respondents' perspectives in a more objective and truthful manner as a result of this conclusion.

Next, we look at the ages of our respondents, which reveals that 52 of them, or 15.7 per cent of the entire population, are under the age of 25. 140 respondents, or 42.2 per cent of the overall population, are between the ages of 26 and 35. Respondents between the ages of 36 and 45 account for 51 per cent of the entire population, or 15.4 per cent. There were no respondents above the age of 55 who took part in the survey. According to the data gathered, the majority of those who took part in this questionnaire survey are between the ages of 26 and 35. Based on the obtained data, all age groups are represented in this survey, and we may be able to learn about each age group's perspective in this survey.

Another factor was education, with 23 respondents having completed senior secondary school, 105 have completed a diploma in hospitality management, 125 have completed a bachelor's degree, and 79 have completed a master's degree, resulting in a percentage of 6.9%, 31.6 per cent, 37.7%, and 23.8 per cent, respectively. The majority of those who took part in the study were either graduates or holders of a hospitality diploma, according to the findings. Graduate and diploma education accounted for 37.70 per cent and 31.60 per cent of our respondents' education levels, respectively, while post-graduate education accounted for 23.80 per cent of our respondents' education levels. We know that the bulk of our responses was well-educated and capable of answering our questions.

Another determinant in our survey was experience or working experience in the hotel industry, with 17 respondents employed for less than one year (freshers), 143 respondents employed for one to two years, 84 respondents employed for two to three years, and the remaining 88 respondents employed for more than five years. According to the data above, the majority of respondents to our questionnaire survey had worked in the hotel sector for one to two years. It demonstrates that the majority of respondents in our poll were knowledgeable and capable of presenting the true image of the sector.

We picked all four regions of India for our survey. 74 respondents worked in hotels in India's northern region, 118 in the western, 60 in the eastern, and 80 in the southern. The vast majority of our respondents hail from India's western regions, with a tiny per centage hailing from the country's southern and northern regions. The eastern region, on the other hand, has the fewest number of respondents (18%).

The nature of employment was one of the deciding criteria in our descriptive analysis. According to the data, 83 per cent of our respondents worked as permanent industrial workers, while just 17 per cent worked on a contract basis. This again shows that we have both types of representation in our survey to know the perspectives of both types of employees.

Our research included working departments, with 71 respondents working in the front office, 72 in housekeeping, 103 in F&B service, 71 in food preparation, and 15 in sales and marketing. We picked respondents who worked in the hotel industry's major operational departments, as described in the previous chapter. Table 4.8 in chapter

4 also displays the per centages of people who responded, which are 21.4 per cent, 21.7 per cent, 31%, 21.4 per cent, and 4.5 per cent, respectively. The table also shows that the majority of respondents are from the F&B service department, with nearly equal numbers from the front office, housekeeping, and food production departments. Because of the severe limits connected with sales and marketing, the sales and marketing department received the least number of responses.

Results display the frequency with which people are eager to work in hotels., the majority of respondents who work in the hotel business are willing to work in the hotel industry with 59.9% and are not willing to work in the hotel sector with 40.1%.

5.2.2 Normality Test

Before we can move on to the analysis, we must first pick which test is appropriate for our data. We were trying to decide between parametric and non-parametric tests, so we used the data from our survey to do a normality test. When skewness and kurtosis are employed to evaluate normalcy, the z-test is utilised. The skew or excess kurtosis values are divided by their standard errors to get a z-score.

Skewness has a z-value of -0.53, which is in the range of -2 to +2, and kurtosis has a z-value of -2.44, which is in the range of -7 to +7. As a result, the data on work satisfaction follows a normal distribution.

The z-value of skewness is 0.38, which is in the range of -2 to +2, while the z-value of kurtosis is -2.48, which is in the range of -7 to +7. As a result, information about an employee's perks is generally disseminated. Skewness has a z-value of 1.30, which is in the range of -2 to + 2, and kurtosis has a z-value of -1.14, which is in the range of -7 to +7. As a result, training and development data is widely disseminated.

The z-value of skewness is -0.46, which is in the range of -2 to +2, while the z-value of kurtosis is -2.29, which is in the range of -7 to +7. As a consequence, employee perception data is disseminated normally. Skewness has a z-value of 1.38, which falls between -2 and +2, while kurtosis has a z-value of -2.25, which falls between -7 and +7. As a result, data on occupational choices follow a normal distribution.

We verified normality on student data as well, and the results were the same as above. Skewness has a z-value of -0.5, which falls between -2 and +2, while kurtosis has a z-value of -2.15, which falls between -7 and +7. As a result, the data of student interns' mean scores follow a normal distribution. It is very much clear that the data gathered through the survey was normally distributed, so we applied a parametric test for further analysis.

5.2.3 Factor Analysis

Factor analysis is a technique for condensing data from a large number of variables into a smaller number of variables. As a result, it is also referred to as "dimension reduction." The "dimensions" of our data have been reduced to just five "components or super-variables." Our data has been separated into five components, as described in Chapter 3, which are job satisfaction, employee benefits, training & development, employee perception, and career choice. The Principal Component Analysis (PCA) method was used.

5.2.4 KMO Test and Bartlett's Test of Sphericity to Check Adequacy Of Sample

The Kaiser-Meyer-Olkin sampling adequacy test is used to examine if partial correlations between variables are moderate. The Kaiser-Meyer-Olkin test value should be more than 0.5 (KMO> 0.5) to establish the validity of the used variables. If the correlation matrix is an identity matrix, the factor model is erroneous, according to Bartlett's test of sphericity. For Bartlett's test, the significance level should not exceed 0.05. (Sig. 0.05).

As a consequence, the validity of the measurement procedures for each content construct will be addressed. The results of the KMO and Bartlett's sphericity tests for the overall construct are shown in Table 30 in Chapter 4. The data set is eligible for factor analysis since the resulting number is more than 0.5, according to the sufficiency and suitability test of data KMO for the execution of factor analysis for overall construction (0.905).

Similarly, the number of significant Bartlett's tests equals 0.01 and is lower than the significant threshold of 0.05, showing that the correlation matrix contains relevant data.

5.2.5 Reliability Test

All of the variables are stable and dependable, according to the findings of the Internal Reliability Test, because their coefficient alpha values are more than 0.90, which is considered exceptionally outstanding reliability. For the coefficient alpha value, job satisfaction earned a score of 0.93, employee benefits received a score of 0.90, training and development received a score of 0.95, employee perception received a score of 0.93, and career choice received a score of 0.95.

5.2.6 Confirmatory Factor Analysis – Structural Equation Modelling

Table 33 in Chapter 4 shows a summary of the variables' model fit. It reveals that the comparative fit index value is 0.95, which is acceptable because the value must be equal to or greater than 0.90, as stated in table 7 of chapter three. The goodness fit index value is 0.86, which is close to 0.90, which is good. In the same way, the adjusted goodness of fit index value is 0.84, which is extremely close to 0.90. The root mean square error of the approximation value is 0.06, which is within the acceptable range; nonetheless, it must be less than 0.08 to be considered excellent. The Normed Fit Index value is 0.91, which is higher than 0.90, indicating that it is acceptable, and the CMIN/DF value is 2.10, which must be less than 5.00. As a result, all of the values are satisfactory, and this model is suitable for future investigation.

5.3 Inferential Analyses

5.3.1 Pearson Correlation Analyses

According to Pearson Correlation Analyses, all of the independent variables (job satisfaction, employee benefit, training and development, and employee perception) showed a significant relationship with career choice. Furthermore, with the exception of training and development, the correlation coefficients of the three independent variables range from 0.41 to 0.70, showing that they have a moderate relationship with the dependent variable. Employee benefits received a 0.44, while job satisfaction received a 0.42. Because training and development have a minor impact on employee career choices, it received a 0.09 score.

Table 5-1: Correlation Value between Independent Variables and Dependent Variable

Independent Variables	Hypothesis	Results
Employee Perception	H_0a: Employees' perception doesn't have a significant impact on their career in 5-star hotels in India. H_1a: Employees' perception has a significant impact on their career in 5-star hotels in India	P-Value = 0.00 (< 0.01)

Employee perception shows a substantial positive link with career choice (r=.44, p 0.01), according to Table 36 in Chapter 4. This correlation coefficient's value of 0.44 falls within the coefficient range of 0.41 to 0.70. As a result, there is a modest link between job satisfaction and career choice. Furthermore, because the p-value of 0.00 is smaller than the alpha value of 0.01, the link between the two variables is significant.

As a consequence, H_0 is rejected but H_1 is accepted, indicating that there is a significant relationship between employee perception and career choice.

Table 5-2: Correlation Value between Independent Variables and Dependent Variable

Independent Variables	Hypothesis	Results
Job Satisfaction Employee Benefits Training and Development	H_0b: Major key factors don't have any significant impact on employees working in 5-start hotels in India. H_1b: Major key factors have a significant impact on employees working in 5-star hotels in India.	P-Value = 0.00 (< 0.01) Job Satisfaction and Employee Benefits (P-Value > 0.01) Training & Development

Job satisfaction shows a substantial positive relation with career choice (r=.42, p 0.01), according to Table 33 in Chapter 4. This correlation coefficient's value of 0.42 falls within the coefficient range of 0.41 to 0.70. As a result, there is a modest relationship between job satisfaction and career choice. Furthermore, because the p-value of 0.00 is smaller than the alpha value of 0.01, the relationship between the two variables is significant.

As a consequence, H_0 is rejected and H_1 is accepted, indicating that job satisfaction and career choice have a substantial positive association.

Employee benefits show a substantial positive relation with career choice (p < 0.01, r=0.44), according to the findings. This correlation coefficient's value of 0.44 falls within the coefficient range of 0.41 to 0.70. As a result, there is a modest relationship between job satisfaction and career choice. Furthermore, because the p-value of 0.00 is smaller than the alpha value of 0.01, the relationship between the two variables is significant.

As a consequence, H_0 is rejected whereas H_1 is accepted, indicating that there is a strong significant relationship between employee benefits and career choice.

Training and development also have a significant positive relation with career choice (p > 0.05), according to the findings. This correlation coefficient's value of 0.09 falls within the range of 0 to 0.20. As a result, there is only a slender or nearly non-existent relationship between training and professional choice.

As a consequence, H_0 cannot be rejected and H_1 cannot be rejected, indicating that there is no significant relationship between training & development and career choice.

Job satisfaction has a substantial positive relation with employee benefits (r=.30, p 0.01), training and development (r=.12, p.05), and employee perception (r=.26, p 0.01), according to the findings. It reveals that work satisfaction has a modest but substantial relationship with employee benefit, a slightly positive relationship with training and development, and yet another minor positive relationship with employee perception.

Employee benefit has a significant positive relationship with training & development (r=.16, p 0.01) and employee perception (r=.26, p0.01), indicating that employee benefit has a negligible correlation with training & development (range 0 to 0.20), and similarly, employee benefit has a significant small positive relationship with employee perception (range 0.21 to 0.40).

Training and development have a minor but substantial relationship with employee perception (r=.20, p 0.01). According to table 32 in chapter 4, there is an almost 20% relationship between these two variables and they lie within the range of 0 to 0.20.

5.3.2 Multiple Regression Analyses

Furthermore, the impact of job satisfaction, employee benefits, training & development, and employee perception on career choice is examined using the findings of Multiple Regression Analyses. With $F_{(4,327)} = 42.18$, p.00, the predictors explained 34 per cent of the variation in the outcome variable with an R2 value of .34. The results reveal that the dependent variable (career choice) and the independent variables (job satisfaction, employee benefit, training and development, and employee perception) have a positive and moderate connection. The R2 indicates how well the independent variables can explain the dependent variable's variations. The coefficient of determination (R square) obtained from this study is 0.34, indicating that independent factors (job satisfaction, employee benefit, training and development, and employee perception) can explain 34% of the variability in the dependent variable (career choice).

Except for training and development, all independent factors were positively predicted, according to the data. Job satisfaction, employee benefit, and employee perception standardised coefficient beta () values are (=.20, p.00, =.30, p.001, =.32, p.000) and training & development standardised coefficient beta () value is (=-.04, p>.05), whereas training & development has a negative and non-significant impact on career choice, while the other three independent variables have a positive and significant impact.

5.4 Variables Affecting Employee' Perceptions Toward the Hospitality Industry as a Career Choice

A T-test is used to identify the variables that influence employee perceptions of the hospitality business as a career option. We looked at the measurements of the connection between a number of variables that might affect existing employees' opinions and attitudes about the sector, as well as their careers in it. Gender, type of employment, and willingness to work in the hotel industry are contingent factors.

The T-test revealed that respondents' opinions of hospitality occupations differed significantly by gender. Female employees have less positive attitudes than male students (mean value=2.74), while there was no significant gender-based difference in students' perceptions of hospitality occupations (mean value=2.60).

There were additional tests to see if there were any statistically significant associations between the respondents' job type (permanent or contractual employees) and their opinions of the sector as a career option. In comparison to those who are permanent workers and on the payroll of the hotel (mean value=2.77), employees who work on a contractual basis in the hotel have a somewhat favourable opinion of a career in the hotel business with a mean value of 2.15. Although there is no major variation in perceptions about hotel careers between the two.

Returning to table 40, the test revealed that the mean value of respondents wanting to work in the hotel sector is 3.16 which is much lower than that of those who are not willing to work in the industry with the mean value of 1.93). It demonstrates that hotel personnel are dissatisfied with their jobs and have a negative or neutral attitude toward their careers.

Similarly, an independent t-test was used to examine the perceptions of hospitality students toward careers in the industry. The results show that male employees have less favourable perceptions (mean value=3.21) than female students (mean value=3.00), but there was no significant gender-based difference in students' perceptions of hospitality careers.

Tests were also carried out to see if there were any statistically significant associations between the respondents' employment experience and whether they had any exposure to industry or not. In terms of their impressions of the sector as a career choice, intern-students who have worked in hotels as interns have somewhat more favourable perceptions (mean value of 3.08) than those who have not worked in the industry as interns (mean value=3.43). Although there is no major variation in perceptions of a career in the hotel sector between the two.

According to the test findings, respondents who were willing to work in the hotel sector (mean value=3.06) had more favourable impressions than those who are not wanting to work in the industry (mean value=3.33). It demonstrates that there is no difference between students who want to pursue a career in the hotel business as interns and those who do not want to seek a career in the hotel industry.

5.5 Conclusion

The statistical analyses on descriptive and inferential analyses of the results from Chapter 4 are summarised in this chapter. Following that, we discuss the findings of our investigation and confirm our research goal.

Chapter-VI

6 DISCUSSION AND CONCLUSION

6.1 Discussion And Conclusions

The present study tries to find the factors associated with hotel's employees and hotel management students' career decisions in the hospitality industry in the Indian region. For the ease of doing research, the main purpose is divided into the following objectives for the research:

- Examining the present perceptions of employees towards the hospitality industry as a career choice.
- To identify the key challenges of employees facing in 5-star hotels in India.
- To identify the major key factor which affect the employees of 5-star hotels in India
- Evaluate the impact of major factors on the perception of hotel's employees working in 5-star hotels.
- Providing a set of specific remedial actions that could be initiated by hospitality stakeholders to improve the image of the industry as a career choice.

6.1.1 Findings & Conclusions On The Basis Of Research Objective – 1:

(Examining the present perceptions of employees towards the hospitality industry as a career choice)

The primary aim of the study was to examine the present perception of employees/students towards the hospitality industry as a career choice. To achieve this objective, various factors were identified from the existing literature as suggested by many researchers. **(Kelley-Patterson and George, 2001; Roney and Öztin, 2007; Ayres, 2006; Ahmad et al. 2009; Penny & Frances, 2011)**. These characteristics were grouped under five major factors Working Hours, Promotion Opportunities, Social Status, Gender Discrimination and Compensation. A structured questionnaire on 5-point Likert Type Scale was designed to examine the present career perception of employees/students in Indian hotels. The data analysis revealed that:

Knowledge: There were thirteen factors identified in this segment. When employees were asked about the factors which they consider important to decide their career decisions. It was observed that the question regarding salary credited on time in the account was one of the important factors which create employee perception with the highest mean score of 3.21 followed by effective leadership (3.17) and appreciation for your contribution (3.13). However, factor proper workload (3.05), other factor promotional opportunities are again coming as important factors during the survey with 3.02 mean value. work enjoyment is having the least important factor with a mean value of (2.96). The findings are in line with previous studies of (**Penny & Frances, 2011; Ahmad et al., 2009).**

It is clear from the finding that employees are influenced by many factors but a few important factors are as discussed above are promotional opportunities, competitive remuneration, reasonable workload. Employees of hotel or students of hotel management consider hospitality jobs as a career if the industry takes care of employee requirement, pay competitive salary on time and allot work as per labour law. The hotel industry is a labour incentive and 24 * 7 running industry.

6.1.2 Findings & Conclusions On The Basis Of Research Objective- 2:

(To identify the key challenges of employees facing in 5-star hotels in India)

This objective tries to find out to identify the key challenges employees face in 5-star hotels in India. The hotel business is facing bigger hurdles than ever in hiring competent and motivated employees than the economy's developing industries **(Kelley-Patterson & George, 2001)**. Although the tourist sector can provide new job possibilities, according to Roney and Ztin (2007), it is frequently accused of supplying largely low-skilled and low-paying positions. This industry has a bad reputation and a lack of comprehension of the potential available **(Ahmad et al., 2009; Kusluvan and Kusluvan, 2000; Aksu and Koksal, 2005)**

Knowledge: As per extensive literature review, Major key challenges were identified which employees are facing in the 5-star hotels in India are as below:

Low Paying Jobs: This is one of the biggest challenges faced by employees that this industry is paying very less to their employees. We have collected data from the employee who were working in various departments on different designations. Employees don't matter on which position they are, mostly employees reported that due to low compensation they feel demotivated and looking for a job change. Employee perception regarding salary that in comparison to other industries, hotel industry pay much less salary.

Poor Image of Industry: Study revealed that the hotel industry in India is carrying a poor image as there are no welfare schemes for employees, Many hotel management students experienced that the industry does not take care of their employees and treat them as labour without any benefits. Employees from management admitted that the industry needs to re-established their image so that employees can find this industry as good for making career and students may also feel motivated to get a job in the industry. By re-establishing a good image, the industry can also come out from the crunch of manpower.

Lack of Opportunities: Our survey also finds out that, the employee is having a set perception that there are no growth prospects in the industry. In the survey, we asked "you got promotional opportunities" and a majority of an employee either were neutral are disagreed. This question was having a 3.02 mean value. Lack of promotional opportunities is again a key challenge.

Work-Life Balance: Our survey shows that employees are facing a problem with their work-life balance. As hotels are 24*7 hours operational industry, so employees have to work day and night. Industry put their employees in different shifts and many of the times employees work in stretched shifts where employees normally work 11-13 hours in a day. Employees also face a challenge to get leaves as limited human resource is available in the hotel. It was observed that the question regarding fulfilling the family requirement was one of the important key challenges which employees face in the industry with the highest mean score of 3.09 followed by a reasonable workload score of 3.05.

Working Conditions: The study shows that working condition in a 5-star hotel is one of the major key challenges. As employees have to work for a longer duration of time and many of the departments where working conditions are not at all good. The housekeeping department is one such department where employees have to use many chemicals which are hazardous for their health, hotel industry does not follow proper guidelines given by governmental organizations result in sickness in employees. On the other hand, Kitchen is one of the areas where employees work in stressful and hot conditions. Employees do not get proper rest during their shift as well.

These findings are in line with the previous studies by **(Ahmad et al., 2009; Kusluvan and Kusluvan, 2000; Aksu and Koksal, 2005).**

6.1.3 **Findings & Conclusions On The Basis Of Research Objective- 3 And 4:**

(To identify the major key factor which affect the employees of 5-star hotels in India and evaluate the impact of major factors on the perception of hotel's employees working in 5-star hotels.)

This objective tries to find out to identify the major factors which affect the employees of 5-star hotels in India. The most important factor identified by respondents was "The opportunity to travel abroad" is having the highest mean value of 3.34 when compared to the other statements which respondents consider very important especially students with industry experience. The second statement 'Job mobility ease to get a job anywhere and 'A job with high quality resources and equipment' are having the second highest mean value 3.30.

Among the statements in this variable, the statement 'A job where I gain transferable skills' had the third-highest mean score of 3.28. The statement "Reasonable workload' has the fourth-highest mean score of 3.23 among these statements. The statement 'Good salary' has the fifth-highest mean score of 3.22 out of all of these statements.

A structured questionnaire on 5-point Likert Scale was designed to identify the major key factors which affect the employee of a 5-star hotel is "Employee Benefits". Employees state that health insurance with the mean value of 2.96 is one of the factors which affect the employees of 5-start hotels positively or negatively. If the hotel provides health insurance to their employee it positively impacts them and positive perception creates among employees. Another factor that affects hotel employees is "Incentives and Bonus" with a mean value of 2.75. If hotels provide timely incentives, performance-based incentives and bonuses to their employee it again affect hotel' employees in a positive manner else employees have a negative perception regarding their job and career in the hotel industry. Respondents admitted that "Child Care Policy" also impact employees especially female employees. This statement in our questionnaire scored 2.73 mean value which is the third important factor as per the survey. The female employee looks for daycare facilities for their children. It becomes more important in the case of a single mother.

One more factor as per our study found important which affect employees is " Gender Discrimination" This study is in line with the prior studies **(Chaudhary and Gupta, 2010); (Russen, Dawson, and Madera, 2021).**

6.1.4 Findings & Conclusions On The Basis Of Research Objective- 5:

(Providing a set of specific remedial actions that could be initiated by hospitality stakeholders to improve the image of the industry as a career choice.)

This study was conducted to determine whether hotel employees and students want to pursue a career in the hotel business and believe that the hotel industry would provide them with the needed career opportunities. According to the findings of the survey, the majority of respondents, including hotel management students, have a strong desire to continue working in the hospitality business. They wish to work in industry after graduation, which contradicts the findings of several prior research such as (Jenkins, 2001) and (Richardson, 2008), but agrees with (Roney and Ztin, 2007).

One of the research goals was to identify a set of specific corrective steps that hospitality stakeholders should do to enhance the industry's image as a career option. The proposals in the following section are addressed to (a) the government, (b) industry employers, and (c) university leaders and educators.

6.1.4.1 The Government

6.1.4.1.1 Government Should Issue Guidelines to Industry for Wellbeing of Employees

As discussed in the chapter 1 introduction, the hospitality and tourism industry is one of the top sectors which has the potential to generate more revenue for the government. Many international hotels have started their operations in India. Government has to implement strong labour laws in this sector as well so that employee exploitation can be reduced in this industry and people can motivate to pursue their careers in the industry. Government has to draw guidelines for the safe, hygienic and hazard-free working conditions for employees and has to conduct regular Strick audits.

6.1.4.1.2 Government Should Fill the Gap Between the Industry and University.

It's vital for the government, which invests a lot of money in hospitality and tourism education, to take efforts to guarantee that graduates stay in the industry when they graduate. As a result, the government, notably the Ministry of Tourism, must reduce the gap (the period between graduation and a student's first job in the hotel industry). Students may not be able to enter the profession during this time and end up working in other professions. This may be achieved by developing a team devoted to connecting fresh graduates with recruiters in the hotel industry. As a result, graduates may be allocated to the top hotels each year to fill open vacancies.

6.1.4.1.3 Establishment of the Hospitality Managers and Educators Collaborative Forum.

The goal of this forum is to foster a long-term, mutually beneficial relationship between industry professionals and educators. It will greatly assist in the planning and implementation of internship practises by highlighting flaws and pointing to ways to close the gap between educational theory and actual practice.

6.1.4.1.4 General Tourism Awareness Activities.

This might take a variety of forms, including informative campaigns, organising speeches by famous industry experts, obtaining authorization to conduct educational field visits to hospitality firms, and enrolling students and graduates in training programmes.

6.1.4.2 The Industry Employers

The hotel industry must continue to work on improving many aspects of the working conditions within the industry. Management must revise their employee salary and motivate them by offering performance-based incentives. The minimum percentage must be fixed for increments in salary. Employers should also focus on the timely release of salary into employees' accounts. How employer is taking care of their employee creates perception and build an image of the industry. To keep this point, employers must provide basic benefits to their employees such as health insurance, meal on duty, pick and drop facility and daycare facility for a child. Employers must establish clear guidelines for sexual harassment and employee must be confident about the safe working premises.

Students say the hotel industry lags behind other industries in a variety of aspects, including compensation, advancement chances, career prospects, and work security. The industry will continue to lose highly qualified and trained workers until it can change the views of a career in the business.

Industry companies are also urged to aggressively seek partnerships with universities in order to establish internship programmes for hospitality students that provide beneficial experiences for students. This results in a win-win situation that benefits both sides.

6.1.4.2.1 Word Of Mouth from Graduated Students.

Word of mouth from students who started their careers in the hotel industry has a key influence in moulding student perceptions of the industry, indicating that there is likely a spillover effect among undergraduate students. As a result, hotel managers must exercise caution while dealing with newcomers, as their judgments of the company might have a considerable influence on prospective recruits' perceptions.

6.1.4.3 University Leaders and Educators

6.1.4.3.1 Tours To Local Hospitality Establishments Must Plan.

Regular field excursions to important hospitality facilities should be planned by the faculty council, in collaboration with local industry experts, so that students may obtain a feel of the business's true characteristics. Educators must help students develop realistic expectations regarding the kind of employment available in the industry, as well as income levels, promotion opportunities, and career paths. They will need to work more closely with industry partners while building future courses.

6.1.4.3.2 Students at universities are technology savvy

With the right plan and preparation, the internet and social media might be utilised to disseminate knowledge and generate interest in the area. The faculty should encourage the development of an innovative and interesting online website aimed particularly at tourism students and graduates. The major purpose of this website is to make it easier for students, teachers, and industry specialists to communicate with one another.

6.1.4.3.3 Enhance the image of hospitality education and show its inherent characteristics

Unfortunately, a significant portion of Indians has a negative perception of people who work in the hospitality industry. They think that everyone, including those with less formal education, may work in hospitality. Hotel management institutions and universities should work to change this negative perception of the hotel industry by demonstrating the real benefit and distinctiveness of such an educational experience.

6.2 Limitation of the Study

One of the thesis's limitations is that it solely considers the impact of 5-star hotel professionals' (employee and students) perception on career progression and the elements that influence their career decision making in the Indian hotel sector. It excludes other factors of the hotel business that might have a detrimental influence on staff performance, such as guest types, customer attitudes, lack of cash available to hoteliers, hotel location, and so on. Another limitation is that it is only focusing only a few hotels from selective cities in India. This study does not touch other category hotels and its main focus is only on 5-star hotels of India. Another limitation of this study is that it only talks about employee and students career perception and do not talk about customer perception or other stakeholder perception.

6.3 Recommendations for Future Research

Despite the limits that we discovered while performing this research, our study can still be completed, and we can present some advice for future researchers that are interested in this area in order to enhance this study.

We explored the link between employee and student perspectives of career choice in four dimensions: work happiness, employee benefit, training and development, and employee perception in this study. The four dimensions we considered might not be enough to show that there are substantial influences on professional choice. As a consequence, we highly advise future researchers to include more independent variables in their studies in order to guarantee that their research is capable of studying this issue from several angles, resulting in more accurate results.

Following that, we were worried about the difficulty we had in obtaining information from our responders. Despite the fact that we employed a filter approach to disseminating our surveys to hotel staff and HM students, there was still a lack of complete viewpoints from our respondents, and they exhibited certain conservative tendencies when giving us their ideas. As a result, we recommend that future studies employ more than one approach for distributing surveys or collecting data from respondents.

Aside from that, we urge that future studies develop a mediating mechanism between hotel professionals' perceptions and career choices in order to make the link between employee/student perceptions and career development more obvious and well understood.

Finally, future studies on this problem in India should include larger coverage regions. The findings of this study will be more indicative of the perceptions of hotel employees across India. We hope that the following proposal will be applied to future research in this sector.

6.4 Conclusion

This chapter also discusses managerial implications to make our study useful to policymakers and practitioners in companies. This chapter also discusses the limitations that may develop when doing this study. Finally, recommendations are made in order to better future research.

The results of our research demonstrated that hotel workers' perceptions have a substantial favourable association with job choice as a conclusion of this study. Job satisfaction, employee benefit, training and development, and employee perception are examples of employee perceptions that may be used to form linkages with career decision making or career choice in the hotel business. As a consequence, the findings of our study may be used as a guide for forming employee and student career perceptions for career decision-making in India's 5-star hotels. Finally, the findings of our research may be utilised as a starting point for future research on employee perceptions of careers and hotel management students' career choices.

www.ingramcontent.com/pod-product-compliance
Lightning Source LLC
LaVergne TN
LVHW010216070526
838199LV00062B/4605